such a long :

CHINESE VOICES IN l

©Ethnic Communities Oral History Project
1994

ETHNIC COMMUNITIES

ORAL HISTORY PROJECT

We are a voluntary organization with a
management committee composed of members
from ethnic community organizations in the
London Borough of Hammersmith and Fulham. It is
assisted by grant funding from Hammersmith and
Fulham Council and other sources.

Our aim is to promote the experiences of people
from the ethnic communities by making them
accessible to as wide an audience as possible. We
are also committed to recording and publishing in
the mother-tongue.

PUBLICATIONS

Hammersmith & Fulham Community History Series:
No.1 The Irish in Exile - Stories of Emigration
No.2 Passport to Exile - The Polish Way to London
No.3 In Exile - Iranian Recollections
No.4 The Motherland Calls - African-Caribbean Experiences
No.5 The Forgotten Lives - Travellers on the Westway Site
No.6 Xeni - Greek-Cypriots in London
No.7 Ship of Hope - The Basque Children
No.8 Aunt Esther's Story
No.9 Sorry, No Vacancies - Life-stories from the Caribbean
No.10 Asian Voices - Life-stories from the Indian Sub-continent
No.11 Sailing on Two Boats - Second Generation Perspectives

Also, on audio-cassette
True Voices of Women Coming to Britain
And on VHS video
The Somali Sailors

Shepherds Bush Library, 7 Uxbridge Road,
London W12 8LJ Telephone 081-749 0982

Acknowledgements
This book was published by the
Ethnic Communities Oral History
Project in 1994. We would like to
thank the following people for their
help in making this book possible:
Christine Mak, Leader of Project
Kiu Wah, Westminster Social
Services, who researched, tran-
scribed, edited and translated the
material, Sav Kyriacou, Co-
ordinator of the Ethnic Communities Oral History Project, Pauline
Savage of the H&F Equalities Unit
for her support, advice and guid-
ance, Jerome Farrell for his proof-
reading of the English section,
Peggy Kwok for her proof-reading
of the Chinese section, Susana
Chung for her patience and accu-
racy in typing the Chinese manu-
script, Adam Saunders for the cover
painting and special thanks to all
the Chinese people who contributed their life-stories to this book.
Finally, Christine would like to
dedicate this book firstly, to her late
father-in-law and secondly, to her
husband for his undying encouragement and support.
The opinions expressed in this book
are those of the contributors and
are not necessarily shared by the
publishers.

Introduction

Early Chinese seamen began to establish a Chinatown in London's Limehouse district around the 1880's. The majority of them came from Sze Yao, a southern district in China. Some of them jumped ship to search for better paid work and some hoped to register in a British port so as to be paid the same rates as British seamen.

The Chinese seamen that settled in the Docklands soon moved to set up laundry businesses. With a small amount of money and a pair of hands they started their business. However, these early seamen saw themselves as 'sojourners' who, having saved enough money, would return to their home villages in southern China. After the war many did return to China. With the introduction of washing machines, the laundries started to disappear. Those who remained were compelled to find work in a new section of the economy, the restaurant trade. This move into catering provided the foundation for the next phase of Chinese migration to Britain.

The Chinese expansion into Britain is a direct result of both pull and push factors. The pull factor occurred in the late 1950's and early 1960's. Britain's economic boom and a change in eating habits developed a taste for foreign cuisine, mostly Indian and Chinese. The Chinese restaurant trade grew rapidly and in the decade between 1956 and 1966, the rate of immigration rose accordingly. Most of the Hong Kong Chinese came from the New Territories, the rural side of the Colony.

The push force occurred during the same period. A large amount of refugees from southern rural China moved to the New Territories and due to high land rental prices and lack of job opportunities, many decided to go abroad. Furthermore, the industrialisation of Hong Kong and the increase of imported agricultural products from China made the situation difficult even for native farm workers to survive.

With the introduction of the Commonwealth Immigrants Act in 1962, two distinct phenomena emerged. Firstly, as the restriction created more difficulties for Hong Kong born Chinese to enter into the United Kingdom, many restaurateurs were forced to recruit aliens not covered by the Commonwealth restrictions. These labourers were mostly from the southern part of China. Secondly, the tightening of Immigration Acts persuaded many Chinese of the need to call for their families to join them in Britain. These were mainly their wives, children or grandparents.

Today, employment is predominantly in catering, both in restaurants and takeaways. There are also quite a number of professionals who were mostly reared and educated in urban Hong Kong, or who came as students from Malaysia and Singapore. The number of professionals is gradually growing, with the increase of the second generation, who are brought up and educated in Britain, and show the intention to diversify from the tradition of catering work.

Because of the distinct pattern of settlement and the lack of information or actually the lack of initiative from the 'host society' to learn more about the Chinese community, many stereotypes of the Chinese prevail. The Chinese are mostly related to chop suey, food and restaurants. They are quiet, self-contained, unwilling to integrate into British society, politically inactive, disciplined and inward looking. By contrast the Chinese are also related to Triads, drug trafficking and gambling.

Stereotyping can be a very strong controlling mechanism. It labels a group of people under certain generalised characteristics, and thus ignoring the causation and the social conditions that create these circumstances. Furthermore, the real situation and problems faced by the community will then be unrecognised.

By giving Chinese people the opportunity to tell their experiences in their own words, this book attempts to break down these stereotypes, and provide readers with the chance to better understand the Chinese community living in Britain today.

Christine MAK

My name is WONG Yuen Tai. I was born on 14th July 1928 in Hong Kong. My father was a business man and ran a fabric shop. My father had three wives and six children. My first mother died young, my second mother had two children by my father and my natural mother was his third wife. I have two sisters, one step-sister and two step-brothers.

My father died when I was four. My older step-brother and my natural mother left Hong Kong and returned to Tieu Shan, China. My two step-brothers were running two shops and looked after the family. I went to the village school and finished at primary school when I was 13. When the Japanese invaded China there was a lot of bombing in my village and it was very difficult for us to stay in the area. I then went to Siu Kwan with my sisters. We walked for sixteen days before we reached safety. At the age of 16 I joined the military school in the hope of fighting for my own country, and was there for three years. But I did not feel that army life was suitable for me so I then packed up and returned to my homeland. I actually left the army when the war ended.

At the age of 21 I went to Hong Kong to find a job. Life was difficult after the war and a lot of people worked for food only. I worked in various trades, including as a shop-keeper, a chef and an assistant engineer in the China airline workshop. I started a small business in 1950 dealing with foreign trade; it was named On Tai Hang. In 1951 there was a reduction in trade between Hong Kong, America and

Europe and the business went down hill. Therefore I had to close my business and I joined a famous foreign department store called SUN LOK. The store comprised many shops, a hotel and a restaurant. I started as a shop-keeper and worked my way up to being the store manager. I was hard working and a loyal employee, and had gained a lot of trust from my employers. I learnt a lot in the job as I was exposed to a wide spectrum of people.

My mother was a devout Christian and I was very much influenced by her. I believed in God and always attended church with my mother when I was young. As I have to work on Sundays, I find it difficult to attend church so I no longer think of my self as a devout Christian, unlike my mother and sister. My mother was barely literate, but she had read the whole bible. Minster LEE, the first missionary for Chinese people in this country, has been one of our closest family friends for many years.

I met my wife in 1958 in Hong Kong, and I got married when I was 31. Our wedding was a simple ceremony. We went to the register office and only invited a few friends to our celebration dinner. I then left Hong Kong for England on 3rd April 1960, alone, and have been living in this country for more than 33 years. I came to England wanting to seek new opportunities in this country, because the 1960s was a difficult period for many Chinese people to make a living in Hong Kong. In those days not many Chinese wanted to come to England because it was said to be a poor and deprived country.

Comparatively, Chinese people would envy you if you went to America, which was be-lieved to be a 'golden mountain' for making money. People told me that I would not even have potatoes to eat if I came to live in England.

Once I arrived here I felt that England could offer me new opportunities for my life. I came to England by sea and saved enough to pay the fare myself. The journey lasted for almost a month. It was a new starting point for me.

I first came to meet a friend of mine who used to work with me in Hong Kong. She told me that her husband's business was in a real financial crisis and would need to be closed down soon. He was also looking for a partner to finance his restaurant business. I told them that I would try my best to help them. They were delighted to learn that I would raise money to support their business. As I had brought some savings with me to England, I became a partner in their Chinese restaurant. I worked in the kitchen as the chef. I had learnt my cooking skills in Hong Kong when I was working in the restaurant of the SUN LOK department store for three months. Through our hard work the business flourished, and in 1962 I bought the other share from my partner and took over the whole business. In 1965 I opened another Chinese restaurant with a friend of mine in Woking.

In 1969 I lost a lot of money in the business, so I left Woking and moved to a takeaway shop in Hammersmith. I have been living in the area for more than 22 years and have also had a second Chinese restaurant in Woking for three years. Only in 1981, did we extend our takeaway shop in Hammersmith and convert it into a Chinese restaurant.

My first language is Cantonese but I can also speak Toi Shan and Mandarin. As I learnt some English in Hong Kong when I worked in the store, I understand a lot of English and manage to deal with day to day conversation. I feel that English people are kind and they do not mind speaking to me even though I am unable to express myself thoroughly. They forgive me because I am Chinese and English is not my native language. I always say sorry to them when I cannot explain myself properly. Most of the English people I meet are very polite and understanding. Some of them tell me that they do not even speak a single word of Chinese and ask me not to keep apologising. I am not ashamed of not being able to speak fluent English because I am willing to learn and improve myself.

My first impression of England was good. I felt that English people were polite and friendly. English people are very practical and down to earth, and as long as you are hard working and law-abiding, you should not have any problems living here. This country looks after its citizens very well, as we enjoy a free health service and many other benefits. The free education system is wonderful here.

In the 1960s it was easier to get a council flat if you were homeless. Also we did not have to wait for a long time to be admitted to hospital if we were in need of an operation. Pregnant women were well looked after and we also collected our free milk when my wife came to join me with our two year old baby girl. It is a little more difficult now, but the education system is still wonderful. Those children who come from poor families do not have to pay for their education and still get a chance to go on to higher education. The state gives them the opportunity to receive a good education.

I held a British passport when I first came to England and had no problem getting through the immigration control on my arrival. I feel that I have made the best use of my skills in this country and have worked very hard to make a living. So far, I have not joined any union or catering workers' club because I have not had the time to do so.

The British Chinese see themselves as guests living in a foreign land. Of course, there are occasions when I experience racial discrimination from white people, but I always keep quiet and try not to make an issue of it. Some English people refuse to pay their bill for no reason after they have finished their meal in our restaurant. Some of the English customers are very demanding and difficult. I have come across some English people who have cursed and shouted at me to return to China; most of time I try to be patient and tolerate this type of behaviour. My attitude is that we need to avoid trouble and try to forgive them.

Another example of racial harassment that I

have experienced is the unreasonable treatment I have received from my neighbours. I remember the time I bought my first house, my neighbour climbed into my garden and drilled holes into all the trees. I reported it to the police but I was told that I would have to provide evidence for the allegation. Sometimes my son would be playing in our front garden when my neighbour would tell him to go away. They also complained about us making noises at night. Despite my attempts at trying to please them by offering gifts and food I failed to build up a friendship with them.

The British Chinese are passive and quiet because they are afraid of making trouble. Chinese people are politically inactive and are not interested in political power. The first generation of Chinese people living in this country found it difficult to participate in politics since the majority of them are not well educated. I only hope that the second or third generation will be more concerned about our rights and welfare by taking part in elections or joining a political party to represent our own people.

Although I have been living in a foreign country, I still practise some of our Chinese customs and traditions. We always celebrate Chinese festivals, such as Chinese New Year, with my restaurant employees; we gather to have drinks and a big meal on that occasion, and greet each other with good wishes. I also visit my mother's grave twice a year - around Ching Ming and Chung Yeung usually - and take fresh flowers and clear the weeds from her grave.

I have six children. My eldest son is David WONG and he is a graduate in electrical engineering. He went back to Hong Kong in 1981 and works as a Sales Manager for a European electricals company. He travels a lot between China and Europe in his job and comes to see me 3-4 times a year. My eldest daughter is a doctor and graduated from Leeds University. She worked as a general practitioner for a few years and then got married to a Chartered Accountant. She went back to Hong Kong with him and settled there. She is now working for Cathay Pacific Airways as a company doctor and is happily married with a daughter.

My second daughter went to California for her University studies and finished her master's degree. My third daughter is a pharmacist. My youngest daughter has just finished her degree at Cardiff University where she studied accountancy. My youngest son is only 18 years old and still at college.

I feel that the English education system gives a lot of opportunities to those children who have the talent and who like studying, as they have the chance to receive higher education and develop their skills. Free education is available to all, regardless of race and ability.

Bringing up children in this country does not seem to me a difficult task. I spent a lot of time with my children and put all my efforts into providing the best for them. I explained to them and taught them about our Chinese culture and customs. They also mixed with our own Chinese people.

I hope that my children will be useful members of society and will be independent. I put my family first and try my best to fulfil all my responsibilities as a husband and father. All I wish is for my children to be law-abiding, decent, useful members of society, which they are.

I have no plans to return to Hong Kong because I like England. There is a Chinese expression that travellers eventually come to see the place where they have settled as their homeland.

1. What is Ching Ming?

My name is Lai Ngor WONG. I am 72 years old and I was born on 12th May 1921. My place of origin is Shun Tak, China. I had many brothers and sisters but nearly all of them died at an early age. In the old days, Chinese people would have as many children as they could as they would be lucky enough if only half of them survived because of the low infant mortality rate. My parents had 13 children and I was the youngest in the family. I was also the fourth girl so I was given the nickname 'Say Tse', meaning number four sister. I did not understand why my father was always beating my mother but she still had his babies. I asked my mother why she slept with my father even though he treated her badly. I was told not to ask such a stupid question; perhaps my mother really loved my father.

My father died when I was very young. I never received any formal education because we were very poor. However, I learnt to read myself. My parents had never worked and most of my uncles were thieves in the village and stole to make a living. I gathered from my mother that my father drank a lot. He did not steal with his brothers but instead asked for money from them. I still remember some of my uncles carrying guns and robbing all the ships which came near Shun Tak harbour.

I began to work as a maid when I was 14, baby-sitting for rich families. When the Japanese invaded China I escaped to Macau first and then later to Hong Kong. When the war was over, I worked as a servant for many families. I believe I was quite a pretty girl and several young men were keen on me, but I was so arrogant and picky that I never went out with anyone. Therefore I have never married during my life. As a young woman I also had a rather nasty attitude towards young Chinese working class men, looking down on them. I now regret not getting married and having a family. Maybe it was better not to have any children as I am quite free and with no ties.

I have been living in England for more than 26 years and first came here with my employer in 1965, my employer bought the airline ticket for me. My employer was actually the owner of a well-known commercial bank in Hong Kong. I was a servant to this rich family and looked after his three children, who all went to Oxford University. I was a housekeeper at their flat in Paddington and I was responsible for cleaning, washing and cooking for the three children. I used to visit Oxford University to see these children at least once a week, to take all their clothes and the food they wanted to eat.

I was very excited when I first came to England. Although I do not speak English, I managed to find my way to Oxford with clear instructions from my employer. My memory was very good when I was young. I think I have a quick brain and learnt very quickly. At times I did feel lonely, but I was very happy that my employer brought me to live in this country.

Even though I was given an airline ticket every year to go back to Hong Kong for a holiday, I seldom took up the offer as I was not bothered. I later looked after two more children for the family. My first impression of England was good. Life here in England is peaceful and safe.

I do not read and write English but I still try hard to learn to recognise English words. Once I went into a gentlemen's toilet because I could not read the sign. Some of my friends laughed at me but I did not really think it was a big problem. You only learn by making mistakes!

I realised that I was suffering from diabetes a few years ago when I was in Shanghai and then I became very ill and fainted in the bathroom of my employer's house in 1986. My friends told me that I had been in a coma for more than four weeks at St. Mary's Hospital. When I regained consciousness, I had lost my power of speech and the use of the left side of my body. Of course, I could not return to work as a servant and needed someone to look after me. I was told that I had been operated on by the consultants on several occasions before I regained my consciousness. Fortunately, my employer paid for me to go into a private nursing home. I gradually recovered from my illness and regained my mobility after staying there for more than six months.

Following my discharge from the home, I was helped by a Chinese social worker and got re-housed in my present council accommodation on the Lisson Green Estate. Thank God I am still alive. After this serious illness I became a devout Christian and now attend St. Martin's

Chinese church every Sunday.

I have been living in this council flat for more than five years, since 1988. In the first two years I lived on my savings because I had more than ten thousand pounds in the building society. When my savings went down, I approached the Chinatown Chinese Community Centre and asked the worker to help me make a claim for benefits. I am now getting a small pension plus income support.

I have not come across any racial incidents and I feel that English people are very nice to me. I think English children can be quite difficult. I mean those who are referred to as 'hooligans'. There are many young kids sitting on the staircase outside the block where I live. They are very naughty and try to tease me and upset me whenever I walk past them. Although they do not ask me for money, they still make a nuisance of themselves. One day I was walking past the staircase and some young people made fun of me, so I showed them some martial arts with my walking stick. Of course I know these skills because I learnt Kung Fu when I was young in China. They were very surprised to see me doing martial arts and said to me 'very good!' After that incident they never teased me or came near me to pull my hair again. They have become friendly to me now.

Although I have no family or relatives in this country, I have a lot of friends who are willing to help me. I have a god-son whom I met at the airport many years ago. He is 30 and works in Chinatown as a waiter. We became good friends when I was ill. He is now married with two children. He visits me very often to make sure I am getting on all right. He also helped fit my sink and is a handy man around the house. I regard him as my son and will give some of savings to him after I die.

My neighbours are also very nice people and I always say hello to them whenever we meet in the street. I like living in this area and am very happy to stay in this country for the rest of my life. I have now got my British passport and am a British citizen. This country is good to its citizens and I enjoy all its rights and benefits. Sometimes I feel that it is better to have a good welfare system than a son because you always know the welfare system will look after you; and you cannot guarantee that your children will. Of course, I shall continue to live in England.

2. How many animals are used by ancient astrologists in China to denote a cycle of years that people are born?

My name is Franklin CHIN. I was born on the 29th September 1920 in Caledonia, Jamaica. My father had two wives, one was a Chinese whom he had married and left in China before he went to Jamaica, and the other was a native Jamaican. My mother was Jamaican and I had one brother and two sisters. In Jamaica my father ran a grocery shop and in the 1920s you were thought to be quite wealthy if you had a business.

In 1928, my father asked a relative to take me and my ten year old brother back to China while he and the rest of the family remained there. We were taken back to Po On, Canton Province, China, which was my ancestors' place of origin, to live with my father's first wife and my half-brother and half-sister.

We all got on quite well and my Chinese mother treated my brother and me as part of the family. We were sent to the village school where we had three years of formal education before we were sent to work on the land. We all needed to work in the fields and grow our own food and it was fortunate that we grew enough sweet potatoes to feed the whole family. My Chinese mother also took our crops to the market and bartered for other essential items, like rice and meat.

Our peaceful lives were rudely and abruptly interrupted when the Japanese invaded China in 1937. This terrible war caused severe famines in China and during the war life was very difficult and hard, but the family survived. The war between China and Japan lasted for almost ten years, and during this time my Chinese mother lost contact with my father as all correspondence between civilians was stopped and my father did not even know whether we were still alive.

Since I was brought up in China, I followed my Chinese mother in practising traditional Chinese ritual religious ceremonies. For example, I burn incense and worship my ancestors. Therefore, it is not surprising that I met my wife through a matchmaker when I was 26, in a traditional arranged marriage. It was a big ceremony and my Chinese mother had paid a lot of money for this wedding as it is traditional for the groom's family to pay for the whole wedding. We had invited more than 100 guests, mainly from our village, and had a banquet in our honour. During the wedding we performed all the ritual procedures , for instance my wife and I had to kneel down three times and bow nine times to the sky and the ground. As my father was not present my Chinese mother was the head of the family and she made all the decisions for the wedding.

After the marriage, my wife and I continued to work as farmers in China and we had a daughter; but life was still very hard and we were very poor. Our lives took a turn for the worse when the communists came to power in 1949. In 1957 when the political climate was so tense and unstable I decided to leave China to find a better future. As emigration from a communist country was impossible I had to leave my family behind and escape from China through a dangerous route, by travelling over the mountains for many days until I reached Hong Kong. In those days any refugee who had made it across to Hong Kong was allowed to stay. In Hong Kong I went to the Immigration Office and asked them to help me to trace my father's whereabouts in Jamaica. The Hong Kong government was very helpful and eventually found my father's address in Jamaica. I then wrote to my father and he replied by letter and told me that he would try to buy me a ship's ticket to Jamaica so that we could be re-united; but he was no longer running his business and so could not afford to pay for my journey. Fortunately, as I was treated as a refugee, the International Council paid for my journey and I was then able to fly to Jamaica to be re-united with my father in 1959.

When I arrived in Jamaica, my father and my natural mother came to meet me at the airport. Naturally and understandably, I was delighted to see my parents again, but my father was now a very old and weak man. I also wrote to my wife and throughout our separation we kept in touch constantly via the post.

I lived in Jamaica for three years and worked in various grocery shops for my Chinese relatives before I came to England in 1962 with my employer to work in his new grocery shop. For my passage I had to save to pay for my flight to England and I can still remember the ticket cost £80. Since I held a Jamaican passport, I did not need any visa or work permit to come to England. Sadly, soon after I left Jamaica, my parents died.

I first arrived in New Cross in south east London on a cold winter's day in January. It was snowing heavily and I had not brought any thick clothes, so my employer gave me some. The weather was so different from Jamaica where we could always enjoy the sun. I wrote to my wife and asked her to send me a quilt, as it was very expensive to buy one in this country but much cheaper to send one from China. I worked in the grocery shop with another Jamaican, and my employer - who was also my relative - allowed us to live above the shop for a small rent.

I had kept in touch with my wife in China for all these years and sent money home for her to look after the family. In 1963 my wife left China and went to Hong Kong when there was an exodus of Chinese following the Cultural Revolution. My wife managed to find a job in a factory in Hong Kong and our daughter was looked after by a relative in China at that time. I went back to Hong Kong to see my wife in 1969. The main reason for me to go to Hong Kong was to register to get a marriage certificate so that my wife could then come to England to join me. My wife eventually came to England in 1970.

In 1968, I moved to live in Warren Street and worked in Chinatown as a cleaner in one of the Chinese casinos for more than ten years. For the last 20 years, I have been living in various places in Chinatown and my wife has also been working in Chinese takeaway shops outside London. As my wife would often be working away from London she would only come to stay with me on her off days.

Looking back, I liked my job in the casino because it was an easy one and I got lots of tips from the customers. However, my employer never paid any national insurance for me and subsequently I was not entitled to a retirement pension when I retired.

My first language is Hakka. I speak only a little Cantonese and English but I can speak quite a lot of Patois, which is a Jamaican dialect. I have a lot of Jamaican friends in London and I still see them very often. I see myself as Chinese even though I have some Jamaican blood. So far, I have not experienced any racial discrimination in this country. I love to mix with Chinese people and I get on well with white people and my Jamaican friends.

My daughter is now married and living in Hong Kong. She has a son and a daughter. My wife and I go to Hong Kong to see them regularly.

My wife and I still practise some Chinese customs, such as celebrating the Chinese New Year and Moon Festival. Nowadays my social activities are meeting my friends and playing Hakka cards. I have also joined some pensioners clubs and enjoy the outings which are organised by the Chinese Community Centre. Sometimes my close Jamaican friend, Harlen, comes to visit me and I cook a special meal for him, a dish of mackerel with banana sauce as he does not like Chinese food. I see him once in every three weeks and often visit his home in Brixton.

Since I do not speak much English, I go to the Chinatown Chinese Community Centre and Social Services Office for help in dealing with my claim for benefits. I feel that white English people are very nice to our Chinese people. I think that Chinese people have settled in very well in this country and that there are no special problems for the Chinese Community.

My wife and I now live in a council flat in Chinatown. We are being well looked after by the state as we receive state benefits and have no need to worry about money. My wife is now 63 and she looks after me very well. I like to live in the Chinatown area because I can meet my friends, do my Chinese shopping and join in all the social activities which are organised by the Chinese Community Centres in the area.

I have just returned from my visit to Hong Kong. My wife and I spent seven months there. We both wanted to return to this country as the weather was too hot and humid there and I could not sleep and eat well. Although my daughter and son-in-law looked after us very well and wanted us to stay, we feel that we belong in England. I like living in England because the weather is cooler and I am used to the English weather; also, life here is peaceful and comfortable. I believe I will continue to live here for the rest of my life.

3. *What are the two main dialects spoken by Chinese people in Britain?*

My grandmother gave me the name Tim Tai, which means bringing a brother, but my father actually named me So Ha. I was born in Po On, China, in 1920. My mother had given birth to six girls and both my parents would have liked to have had a boy when I was born. I was the youngest girl and three of my elder sisters died when they were infants. I thus have two sisters.

When I was seven my father left China to work in Singapore. My mother and my sisters went to join him when I was ten and I was left at home to live with my grandmother. I came from a very rich family and I was given a mui-sei (personal maid) to look after me.

I started my Chinese schooling when I was eleven. I had to leave school after I had received four years of education. It was a traditional Chinese belief that girls should not be educated because their future would be to stay at home. My elder sister's marriage was arranged when she was only twelve. I was engaged to a boy when I was five.

When I was 15 my parents returned from Singapore, bringing with them a three year old boy they had bought from a poor family. I was told he was my little brother. My parents had also brought another mui-sei to look after my brother. They then went back to live in Singapore.

It was arranged that I should marry my fiancée when I was 20. I was fortunate to have had the opportunity to meet my future husband and correspond with him for a while before we got married. That way I was able to find out about him before my wedding. It was a western-style wedding and I actually wore a white lacy wedding dress and married at a register office in Po On.

I married into a big family and had three mothers-in-law, because my father-in-law had three wives. I was a spoiled child in my family and I never had to do any housework as I was well looked after by my mui-sei. After I got married I was always in tears, because I felt that I was badly treated by my in-laws. I was only allowed to eat the leftovers and had to do all the housework in the house. In those days in China, women or daughters-in-law were treated as second class citizens and held little status in society. I finally stopped crying and feeling sorry for myself after I gave birth to a baby girl at the age of 23.

Two months after our wedding, war between China and Japan broke out. The family had to escape the heavy fighting by moving to South China. When the war was over and the communists ruled China in the 1950s, the rich suffered a lot. Both my family and my husband's family members were badly treated by the red guards as we were 'rich land-owners'. All of our possessions were confiscated by the communists and we had to bury my grandmother without a coffin. My brother managed to escape and hide away in South China. While these tragic events were taking place my parents, who were still in Singapore, wrote to me and said that they were too afraid to return to China. My husband and I then did farm work in the fields for the state and we managed to survive this episode. My husband later was given a teaching job in Tek Mun and eventually left China and went to Hong Kong to find a job in a shoe factory when he was 34. I went to Hong Kong and joined him with my two daughters in 1957.

I became a stronger woman when my husband died at the age of 37; I was 36 years old at that time and worked in a factory to make a living. I came to England in 1976 when I was 55.

It has been 18 years since I came to live with my daughter in this country. I still remember the night when I arrived at the airport. It was a very cold night and the plane landed at 3 o'clock in the morning. I first came to live in Hammersmith with my daughter's family. I did not like England at all because I did not speak any English and stayed at home most of the time. I helped to look after my daughter's two young children and cook for the family. My son-in-law and daughter went out to work leaving me alone with the children. I knew nothing about the outside world and stayed at home waiting for the family to come home every day. I felt very isolated and miserable for most of the time.

It was about ten years ago that I learnt to travel around London on my own and attended English classes in Chinatown. Although I still cannot speak fluent English, I understand a lot and know how to travel on a bus and do my shopping in a grocery shop or in the market.

Since all my grandchildren had grown up, I managed to find the time to meet some Chinese people in the Community Centre. I now come to Chinatown every day and join in the activities organised by the pensioners club.

I found myself not getting on well with the younger generation and felt that I was not happy staying in my daughter's home. I therefore decided to move out and live near Chinatown. I sought advice from a Chinese Community worker who works in Chinatown.

Last year I was helped by a Chinese Social Worker to move into a flat in Soho. It is a one-bedroom flat run by the Housing Association and the block where I live is a sheltered home. The Housing Association has employed a Cantonese speaking porter to look after the Chinese residents, which is really helpful.

My first language is Cantonese and I now speak a little English. I feel the language barrier is still a major problem for most of the older generation of Chinese people who live in this country. I feel that I am very lucky to be fit and well, as I believe there is a need to develop services for those elderly Chinese people who are frail and in poor health. There might be a need to set up an old people's home specially for the elderly Chinese near Chinatown.

So far, I have never experienced any racial incidents and I feel that most white English people are very nice to Chinese people. Most of my neighbours are white. They are very kind to me and every now and then they come to see me to find out whether I am all right. I am very grateful to them for their kindness.

Since I came to live in this country, I have not practised our Chinese traditions and customs. I do not bother to make a Chinese New Year cake or burn any incense. I do not feel that I need to do all these ritual prayers in a foreign country as life is more simple here.

I am keen to meet Chinese people and always join in the activities in the clubs for the elderly. I enjoy listening to Chinese opera and keep many tapes at home. I love reading and calligraphy. I spend my spare time reading Chinese novels. Sometimes I borrow Chinese videos from the Chinese library and invite friends to come to my home and watch them with me.

Having lived in this country for more than 18 years and brought up two grandchildren, I realise that the older generation these days should be more open minded and prepared to accept young people's ideas. I feel that we cannot apply old principles and doctrines to our children. I remember I had to listen and follow every word that my parents said to me. We cannot force the younger generation to listen to our advice. We need more patience with our children and somehow to learn to listen to their views in order to live in harmony with them.

I like the peaceful and comfortable life in England. I have now learnt to live alone. I do not think I will return to live in my homeland, China, in the future as I will continue to live here and enjoy the rest of my life in London.

4. Which London Borough contains the largest Chinese population?

My name is WONG Oi. I was born on 22nd June 1926 in Fu Tin village, Shum Tsan, China. I had three brothers and two sisters. My parents were farmers. I never received any formal education, firstly because my family was poor and secondly because I was not a male. In those days girls were not allowed to study but boys normally had the chance to go to school. Like all farmers' daughters, I helped in the fields and looked after the cows for the family.

My parents died when I was very young. I came to Hong Kong with my aunt when the Japanese invaded China; I was 11 at the time. I stayed with my aunt until I was 15 and then returned to the village in China when the war was over. I later went back to Hong Kong to look for a job because of the difficult times after the war. I worked for many years in a factory which made plastic flowers for export.

I got married when I was 30. I met my husband through introduction by friends. We had been going out for almost four years before we decided to get married. Therefore I was fortunate enough to have the freedom to choose my life partner rather than experience one of the then customary arranged marriages. We went to a register office for our wedding and invited a few friends to our celebration dinner. We then went to Macau for our honeymoon. Since my parents had died, I had to ask my relatives to act as our witnesses for the wedding.

My husband was a skilled shoe maker in

14

Hong Kong in the 1960s. When China started exporting cheap mass machine-manufactured shoes to Hong Kong, the trade went downhill. We had 4 children in 5 years and life was extremely hard for us as we did not earn enough money to feed the children. Often, we adults had to go hungry so that the children were fed. Because of these circumstances, my husband decided to look for other opportunities. Fortunately, my husband had an uncle who was a former merchant seaman and had jumped ship to settle in the north east of England, who applied for a work permit for my husband to work in his Chinese restaurant in Newcastle. My husband left Hong Kong in 1964 and supported the family by sending his weekly wages to us.

When my husband went to England we were living on Hong Kong island in rented accommodation. Following a fire in the building, we were to be rehoused by the Hong Kong Government in Chia Wan, but meanwhile we built ourselves a temporary wooden hut. This temporary accommodation lasted for four years before we were rehoused in a high rise council block. We stayed in this council flat for another three years before we eventually came to England.

In 1971 the family left Hong Kong for good. We came to England by plane but my husband only managed to save up half of the fares, so he had to borrow the rest of the money from his cousin. I remember the journey lasted a long time as we spent more than 20 hours on the plane. The children were very excited to be going to England but nearly all of them were air sick on the plane.

My husband was earning about £7 a week when the family came to join him in England. Life was pretty hard. We lived in rented accommodation and we paid £4.50 a week rent. The youngest child was seven at that time, and I spent all my days looking after my four children since they were still very young and needed me. The eldest one was 12 and the other three were 10, 8 and 7 at that time. Since my husband did not earn enough to pay all the bills, I went to work part-time in a takeaway shop when the children were a little older. I made £6 a week working in the kitchen peeling potatoes. I worked only in the morning, after I had taken the children to school. We struggled to make a living and feed the children.

My husband had been working as an assistant cook in various Chinese restaurants. He learnt his cooking skills from his friends and was gradually promoted to be the chef. He worked for various relatives until he became unemployable because he was said to be too slow to work in the restaurant. By that time we had saved up some money to buy a takeaway shop and we then ran our own family business.

My first impression of England was that it was bitterly cold. It was such a big change in the first place. We did have a difficult time during the first few years we were settled over here. We came across white people shouting 'Chinkies' and throwing stones at us. Of course, there was racial discrimination. We have to keep quiet and try not to get into trouble by leaving the scene as soon as we can. Since we cannot speak the English language and live in someone else's country, we have to be more tolerant. So far, it has only been white children who behaved in this way and I have never been badly treated by adult English people. I suppose children can be ignorant and unenlightened, so we should forgive them.

In the beginning I did not speak any English and it was very difficult for me to talk to people. I can now speak simple English to get by and do my own shopping, and I can also get around by bus.

I have struggled to make a good life for my children. They are now all grown up and most of them have finished higher education. My eldest daughter is married to a Chinese chef with two children and is now living in London. I go to visit her every summer.

My eldest son worked as a laboratory technician in a hospital for more than six years after he finished his degree. He mainly examined blood samples in the laboratory. He was so keen to improve himself and went back to university to study physiotherapy. He has just finished the three year course in June and has already found a job in Sunderland General Hospital. He wants to study acupuncture next year. I think he is a clever boy and he has done very well at school and college. He is now 32 years old and still single. I do wish that he would get married soon. So I have been asking

friends to introduce a Chinese girl to him. He is working so hard now and it seems to me that he is not keen to find a life partner at present.

My second son worked as a social worker in London after he graduated from university. I do not know much English and it is very difficult for me to tell you exactly where he works. This son is now studying a part-time course in law and he wants to be a solicitor in a few years time.

My youngest daughter has finished her degree and has also done a master's degree. At university she met a Hong Kong Chinese boyfriend and after she had finished her studying she went to Hong Kong with him. This young man is a civil engineer working in Hong Kong. This youngest daughter is now working in a local hospital as a laboratory assistant. They are planning to get married early next year.

I worry less these day because all my children have done very well and are independent. I have no need to tell them what they should do. It seems that they know how to plan for themselves. All along my husband and I worked hard mainly for the sake of our children. We wanted them to have the chance to receive a better education and were prepared to give them the best. I never asked my children to work for long hours in our takeaway shop as I always asked them to put their studying first and wanted them to do well at school. Their future will depend on whether they are given the chance to study further . I do hope that they will all be able to have a good life without needing to worry about money.

Although none of my children were born in this country, they can all speak Cantonese. I feel extremely pleased and fortunate that my children have achieved good results in their studies. I have come across some relatives' children who were born in this country but have never been able to go to university because they did not do well academically. I am actually very proud of my children. I have always reminded my children that the only way to leave the family catering business and manual work is to study for higher education and increase the chances of getting a better job.

I often tell them about the hard time their parents went through before we came to England. Thank God that my children are obedient and intelligent. They have never mixed with the bad people and know how to distinguish what is good for them. I love my children very much but try my best to discipline and guide them in the right direction. Of course, I am always there to give them the support and encouragement they need.

My husband and I sold our takeaway business and retired five years ago. We managed to buy our own house and save enough for our retirement. Very sadly, my husband died of lung cancer two years ago and I am now left on my own, living with my eldest son, but I frequently come to visit my daughter in Fulham in London.

I believe in Buddhism and still practise most Chinese customs in this country. I worship our ancestors and burn incense to show them my respect. I stick to my own religious beliefs but allow my children to go to churches and do whatever they want. I still follow a lot of Chinese traditions. We celebrate Chinese New Year, the Moon festival, Ching Ming and Chung Yeung. Since my husband died, twice every year my family goes to visit his grave. We take fresh flowers with us and always gather to pay our respects to him. At home, we prepare a present of a cooked meal, and burn incense in front of my husband's picture. It is only me who practises all these rituals in the family. I do not expect my children to do the same since they were brought up in a western culture and will do things differently. I believe all that matters is that ritual worshipping should be practised genuinely and that our respect should come truthfully from the heart.

I am quite an active member of a club for the elderly in Newcastle. I attend their weekly meetings and join in the activities which are arranged for the pensioners, but not as often as I used to because I suffer from arthritis in my feet and find walking long distances difficult.

Chinese people in Britain are hard working and conscientious. Most of them work for our own Chinese people and not many of them can find a job working for English people. The Chinese people who came here during the early years do not speak much English. I seldom see Chinese people claiming unemployment benefit because we feel ashamed of getting help from

English people. Only those who cannot help doing so because of sickness and old age claim benefits in order to survive. Otherwise not many Chinese people rely on state handouts. Some of my friends retired early at the age of 62 or 63 and claimed benefits. They were obliged to do so because they became unemployable through suffering from ill health and could not continue to work for long hours in restaurants.

Some Chinese people still continue to work after they have reached the age of 60 but are paid at lower wages because they, unlike the young ones, cannot do the heavy manual jobs necessary in the catering trade. The majority of my Chinese friends saved enough money to run a takeaway shop in their late 50s and early 60s. They are mainly running family businesses with all the children giving a hand to make a living.

The second generation of Chinese people who have received a higher education can probably find jobs working for English people. Some young Chinese people still continue to run their family businesses and work in the catering trade. My four children are fortunate enough to be amongst the first group.

I am now getting a widow's pension and lead a reasonable life-style at present because my children always give me extra money for my living expenses. Looking back over all these years, I do not regret having emigrated to this country because we did it to give the best to our children. I am now used to the weather and life here in England. I would not return to China or Hong Kong because I am too old now and do not have much longer to live. I am quite content to live in England for the rest of my life because I am satisfied with my life here.

5. *The most popular and important festival that Chinese people celebrate is Chinese New Year. Why do Chinese people celebrate New Year?*

My name is YUE Kai Chung. I was born on 13th November 1928 and I am now 65 years old. My birth place is Wei Chau, China. My parents had thirteen children and I am the youngest son in the family. My parents died when I was 5 years old and I was brought up by my eldest sister-in-law. My eldest brother is eighteen years older than me and I see my brother and his wife as my parents.

All my family were farmers. We grew sweet potatoes and rice to earn a living. Since my family was very poor I never had the chance to have a formal education and therefore I cannot even read Chinese. I began to earn a living by working as a shepherd for other people in another village when I was 9 years old. When I was 13, my eldest brother asked me to return home and help in the fields. I decided to leave home and go to Hong Kong at the age of 15. On my way to Hong Kong I met some friends who lived in my village and they told me that no one would give me a job and I would probably starve to death because I was too young to look after myself. I then gave up my journey and returned to the village.

When I was 16 I went to Kwai Chau, Szechwan, and worked for some farmers during the harvest seasons. I met my wife, Ah Fung, there in the fields. She was the daughter of the leader of the village and came from quite a well-off family. I knew that she liked me but I did not dare to go out with her because I was a poor labourer working for the landlord. There would be no future for her in going out with

me but of course I was also very fond of her.

She would keep coming to the fields and looking at me from far away. I worked very hard, and one night when I had caught a cold she saw me sleeping under the trees looking very ill, and asked her mother to bring me some sweet potato soup. I was later invited to her house to have a meal with her parents. I was embarrassed and shocked when her parents told me that their daughter liked me a lot and they asked me to marry her. I did not know what to do at that time and did not know how to respond to their request because I was afraid that I was too poor to be their son-in-law. I was also worried that I would be unable to provide her with a decent standard of living.

Fortunately, her parents did not mind that I came from a rural background and told me that as long as I was prepared to work hard we would not starve. I then took Ah Fung with me and returned to my village to see my eldest brother and ask for his permission to get married. Ah Fung was so delighted and excited to come home with me. When my brother saw her he agreed we could marry straight away. Ah Fung was just 14 at that time. In those days boys and girls got married at a very early age. The average age for young people getting married was 13-14.

Our wedding was a traditional one. We had to hold our ceremony at our ancestors' temple in the village. My eldest brother spent a lot of money on my wedding and we invited more than 90 people from the village for a celebration dinner. After our wedding, Ah Fung came to live with my family. We stayed in separate rooms for almost a year before we slept in the same bed and only consummated the marriage when we were 18 and 19 years old. At one time she lived in the room were the rice was milled and I slept in the living room. We were still very young at that time, knowing nothing about married life, and were too shy to make a move.

All along I had been working in the fields for my brother. I eventually left Wei Chau for Hong Kong when I was 20 years old, leaving my wife behind in China. I had always wanted to leave the village and see the urban life of Hong Kong. I took with me three pounds of rice, four duck's eggs and a pair of shoes made of straw. The whole journey took four days on foot before I reached Hong Kong. I spent the nights at open tea bars and slept on benches. It rained heavily on the first night and I thought about my leaving home and arriving in a foreign place without any friends or relatives. I was in tears.

Fortunately, I met a good and kind person, Mr Yung, who guided me all the way past the border between China and Hong Kong at Man Kam Road. He took me with him and I stayed at his house in Hong Kong on my first night there. I still remember the night I had that meal at his place. Since I had not eaten for several days, I very much enjoyed the dish of pork casserole with beetroots. I ate so much that I thought I would die of over-indulging.

When I first arrived in Hong Kong, relatives from the same village as mine found me a job picking vegetables in the fields in Tsuen Wan. When I worked in the vegetable fields, I was scared to death seeing all the worms wriggling around my feet. I actually worked in the vegetable fields for two months and then I moved up to the top of the hill, Tai Mo Shan, to cut bamboo sticks to sell them in the market. Life was pretty hard at that time. I remember that after collecting a bunch of bamboo sticks I got only three Hong Kong dollars (equivalent to about 30 pence these days) for them. I would save up seven Hong Kong dollars, then send five dollars to my wife in China and keep two dollars for food.

It was 1945 when I arrived in Hong Kong, just after the war. There were riots everywhere and street fights between the Kuomintang (the nationalists) and the communists. The Hong Kong governor, Colin Hung, dealt with the situation tactfully and took control to restore order.

I could not make a living by selling bamboo sticks and thus went to various shops and stores asking for a job. I eventually found one working as a coolie on a construction site and as a stone cutter, travelling by lorry. It was really hard work on the building sites. I later returned to work on the vegetable farms in the New Territories. I kept in touch with my wife and always remembered to send money home, and eventually saved enough to buy a small piece of land to farm.

In 1952 my wife came to Hong Kong to join me. She had two sons by me. She did not like the way of life in Hong Kong and later returned to China with my two boys. I continued to send money home to provide for the family.

One of the farm owners I met in Hong Kong, Mr Chung, realised I was a hard working fellow and invited me to come to England to work in his Chinese restaurant. He was a landlord with a lot of land and farms in the rural part of Hong Kong. He came from Wei Tau and was quite rich at that time. I understood that he ran a number of Chinese restaurants in England and wished to recruit some assistants to go over there. Following my agreement, he organised all the necessary papers and bought me an airline ticket to come to England. The ticket cost him about £340 at the time. I finally came to England in 1964.

I went straight to work in the kitchen in Mr Chung's restaurant in Chinatown when I first arrived. I was not paid for the first three weeks as I was told I was an apprentice and would have to work for no wages; I was later paid £5 a week. It was a difficult adjustment for me as I spoke no English at all. I had to rely on other people all the time and thought about leaving the job and going back to Hong Kong, but as I did not have the money to buy the air ticket I told myself that I had better stay to try my luck.

In the 1960s people who held work permits had to report to a police station regularly. I also had to seek permission before I changed my employer in 1968. For all these years I worked as a chef until I became ill in 1986. As I cannot even read or write Chinese, I had to remember by heart how to cook the dishes when I was first learning to be a Chinese chef. Fortunately, many of the friends I made here helped me write letters to keep in touch with my two sons in China after my wife died in 1965. I have never stopped sending money to China, even after all these years.

Life here is quiet boring and monotonous at times. When I was working I spent my one day off from work a week sleeping and sitting in the cinema all day. Since I cannot read and write Chinese, it was difficult for me to learn English, so I was only able to socialise and work with Chinese people. I seldom gambled my salary because I needed the money to send to my family; but sometimes I do feel ashamed of not having been able to save enough and retire to China.

I eventually retired early at the age of 58 because I was suffering from severe arthritis and was unable to work. When I became ill six years ago I was made redundant and was asked to leave the tied accommodation which was provided by my employer. I was fortunate enough to be rehoused by the Council with the assistance of a Chinese community worker. I have been living in this bedsit for more than six years and receive state benefits.

I am satisfied with my present life here in England. Although I am all by myself here, it is much better than returning to live in China since here I have no need to worry about money and I have a place to live. I am now saving up some money to go back to China to visit my sons and grandchildren. My two sons have received more than a thousand pounds from me to build a big house for the family in the village. I wish to see this house for myself.

I like England because this country looks after its residents very well. We enjoy a free health service and the frail and the sick can survive on benefits. I do not want to leave this place now, after all these years of struggling to earn a good living.

Of course, there is racism, but I think English people treat ethnic minority people very well. We are only guests living in a foreign land and we should be grateful for what we get from the English government. I now spend most of my time at home and seldom use my telephone because I have no one to contact in this country. The telephone was installed by Social Services for me to contact my family doctor in an emergency. I have very few friends and seldom join in the activities which are organised by the community. I watch television and am not afraid of being alone in my flat. All these years I have been working and living in Chinatown, so I know the place well; therefore it is very convenient to live near Chinatown. I shall continue to live in England until the day I die.

6. What is the traditional colour a Chinese bride often wears for her wedding?

My name is LEE Wai Ping. I was born on 10th January 1926 at Hung Hum, Hong Kong. My mother had 13 children but some of them died when they were infants and only seven survived; I am the oldest one.

I came from quite a wealthy family. My grandfather ran a construction business in the 1920s, but he died when I was six. After my grandfather's death, my father did not work for three years and later had to sell all our property so we could survive. My father refused to work for low wages and used up all my mother's savings. He graduated from Wah Yan College, which was a famous school in Hong Kong at that time, and he could read and write both English and Chinese. He gave up studying after he got married.

My father later went to work as an inspector for the Hong Kong Electricity Company. His take-home pay was one hundred Hong Kong dollars a month, which was considered to be quite a high wage at that time. My mother was a housewife but she loved playing mah-jongg all day, and was addicted to gambling.

Since my grandfather agreed to give the girls the chance to have an education, I was able to go to school at the age of five. I went to a Catholic school. On my first day at school I received many presents from family, friends and relatives. I also had to eat spring onion, which symbolises 'Chung Ming', meaning intelligence. My family kept many servants in the house and we were well looked after and taken to school by them.

I received only three years of formal education and left school because my mother refused to pay the school fees for me after she lost all her money through gambling. I was said to be a bright girl and had done very well at school. After school I used to play with my brother on various building sites. I was regarded as rather a 'little terror', always getting my own way!

At the age of 12, I began working for my cousins in a printing workshop. I helped do the colouring of the Christmas cards for export. I worked for a few months and made 15 Hong Kong dollars a month. I remember I gave five dollars from my wages to my grandmother to buy cigarettes. I was scared that my mother would find out because I was told that I had to give all my wages to her.

I later worked in a factory which made plastic boots in Hung Hum. Since I could read and write some Chinese, I was given the job of foreman, supervising a group of workers, at the age of 15. The factory owner actually taught me to use an abacus. I was able to do simple calculations and prepare the general wage accounts. I was said to be a hard working and responsible worker.

In 1941 the Japanese bombed Hong Kong. I remember that I was preparing the accounts one day, I was asked to leave the factory as soon as possible. The factory closed down and the owner gave us some rice and told us not to return to work.

Life was really hard during the Japanese occupation of Hong Kong. We had no money and no food. It was very difficult for such a big family as ours to escape and leave Hong Kong. I remember the Japanese soldiers kept searching the houses of civilians; one day they came to our house to look for British troops. Since my father can speak English, he was able to convince the Japanese that we were civilians. Having seen so many young children living in our house, the Japanese soldiers later gave us a bag of rice to feed them. We managed to cook rice porridge to feed everyone for many days. My father and I also went to Kai Tak airport and helped the Japanese to move all the rubble after the bombing. We were given one pound of rice for a day of hard work. We had to use the furniture as fuel for cooking the porridge. Looking back at the war time, which lasted for three years and eight months, we were very lucky to survive.

I also worked for the Japanese soldiers as a maid or servant, to get more rice to feed my brothers and sisters. I managed to get 24 pounds of rice a month working for the Japanese. Without all this rice my family would probably have died of starvation. Fortunately, we managed to stay alive.

When the war was over in 1945, my father was able to find a job working for the water company. I continued to work as a maid for various families and also for the British soldiers. I thus met David, the future father of my daughter, in 1947 in the British barracks. David was a British soldier and had fought in Burma during the war. He could speak some Cantonese. At that time, British soldiers were not allowed to marry local Chinese girls. Once his commanding officer learnt that David wanted to marry me, he was transferred immediately back to England. He left Hong Kong before my daughter was born in 1947. I was 21 years old at that time.

My father had met David and gave his permission for us to get married. Unfortunately, there was no marriage and I was deserted by this British soldier; I have not kept in touch with him. However, I did see him once in London; he probably did not recognise me and I did not go forward to greet him. After all, there was no point of initiating any contact with him.

I brought up my own daughter all on my own. Although my mother had asked me to marry a Chinese man, I did not think it would be a good thing for my girl since she would have been seen as an illegitimate child and would have been rejected for her Eurasian features. In those days single parents were discriminated against and no one would pity you if you were an outcast.

In order to make more money, I worked as a hostess in night clubs. I left the job because the Triad wanted to force me into prostitution. I then found a job in a children's home, working as a nanny in Kowloon. I loved this job because I enjoyed looking after a group of orphans and helping them to create their own future. I stayed in that job for almost 20 years.

In 1972 I came to England to join my daughter, who had married an Englishman two years before and lived in Dover. I still remember going into the Hong Kong immigration office for an interview. I was told that my son-in-law had filled in an application for me to settle in England. I told the immigration officer that I did not really want to come to England because I was so afraid of such a big change in my life. The immigration officer explained to me that I could always return to Hong Kong if I wanted to. He told me that he was surprised to find me so honest, and tried to comfort me. I was soon given a visa to enter the country with the right to settle here permanently.

Once I arrived in England, my son-in-law - who was also a British soldier - was transferred to Singapore for two years. This time I refused to go with my daughter's family and decided to stay with my brother, who lived in Croydon. I later found a job working as a servant for a Singaporean Chinese family and lived in the Paddington area.

Since I did not understand English, I was always given the taxi fare to go to Chinatown by my employer whenever I was asked to do shopping for Chinese things. I was also given a piece of paper with my home address and destination to show to the taxi driver. I always seemed to come across taxis drivers who cheated and refused to give me the change. In those days it cost only 5p to go to Chinatown from Paddington by bus. I used to get so angry that I became determined to learn some English in order to travel around on my own in London.

I worked as a servant for the same family for sixteen years. After retiring from work, I moved to live in a council flat on the Lisson Green Estate.

My daughter's family now live in England. My son-in-law has left the army and found a job working for the BBC. They bought a house in Kent, towards which I contributed £13,000 from my savings. I often see my three grand-children and take them out to Chinatown for dim sum.

I have been living in England for more than 20 years and I like it here because I am not treated as an outcast. In the 1960s, Hong Kong Chinese people did not accept inter-racial relationships. My two sisters married English-men and my father's second wife was also an English woman. I feel that I have no need to hide my background and can be open about my life.

I do not think racial discrimination is a serious problem in this country. I get on very well with my English neighbours and also go to the local Age Concern Day Centre to play bingo with them. I spend most of my time wandering around the market and visiting my friends. I collect my weekly pension and this means I have no need to rely on my children for money. I am very happy and satisfied with my life, and will continue living here for the rest of my life.

7. Every year the fifteenth day of the eighth lunar month is the mid-Autumn Festival in China. It is also called 'Moon Festival'. What is the meaning of it?

Most people call me Mrs MAN. I was born in 1955 in Hong Kong. There were 5 children in my family and I was the fourth child. My father was an office clerk and my mother was a housewife. My family lived on Lantau island for some years before we moved to Hong Kong.

I first attended school when I was seven. I studied up to form II in college and left school at the age of 15 because I was not interested in carrying on studying. My main interests then were in playing basketball and in make-up. I always wanted to join the police force when I finished school but later gave up this idea because my parents objected to me becoming a policewoman. I then worked in various depart-ment stores as a sales person.

It is such a long story to tell you how I came to England. I had never thought I would come to England and only after I met my future husband did I realise that I might do so. One day my sister came home and told my mother that her friend's family were coming to Hong Kong from England to look for eligible young Chinese girls for matchmaking purposes. Her friend's parents were actually coming to find a wife for their son who ran a Chinese restaurant in London. Mrs. Man, my present mother-in-law, asked many girls to give her photos of themselves to show to her son. My future husband was not particularly interested in those girls who had given their photos with matchmaking in mind.

My mother and my sister thought of me and

asked if they could show my photo to this Mr. Man who was said to be in search of a young woman who wished to go abroad. At the age of 21, I had never gone out with any man and had no wish to leave my parents. My parents felt it was time for me to find a life partner. Since I did not object to their suggestion, they gave my photo to Mrs. Man. I then forgot about the whole thing since I did not hear my mother mention it again.

Then one day I was taken by my mother to meet Mrs. Man and her son. It was like love at first sight and I got on extremely well with him. It seemed obvious to everyone at the table that my husband and I liked each other and had a lot to talk about. I also felt that he was such an easy person to talk to and I admitted that I liked him a lot. Naturally we went out together on many occasions. At first, my husband had not wanted to meet the girl his mother was going to introduce him to. He had gone to England when he was 12 and was quite anglicized, but his mother did not wish to see him marrying an English girl and therefore was so keen on matchmaking.

Surprisingly we liked each other a lot and only went out for a very short period (just over a month) before my husband proposed to me. We thus married at the register office and had a reception for our relatives. Once we decided to get married, my husband made an application to the Immigration Office for me to join him in England. My husband was actually running a family restaurant business and he could not

stay in Hong Kong for very long.

He was going to go back first and wait until I got an entry visa to join him. However, everything went very well and I was given the visa to join my husband within two weeks. I then decided to leave Hong Kong with him at the same time. The whole thing happened so quickly that I did not really have time to think about leaving Hong Kong for good and I did not feel anything until I reached the airport on the day I was due to leave. I burst into tears when I said goodbye to my mother. I was so confused and upset when I got on the plane and then realised that everything had been arranged for me and I had not been given the chance to say no. The change was enormous but I had not given any thought to it.

I realised I was the spoiled child of the family, that my mother had looked after me all these years, and now all of a sudden I was miserable and afraid of not being able to cope with a new life in England.

I first came to live with my parents-in-law in Brighton in 1976. My husband worked in central London and only came home once a week to see me. It was quite a big change and I did not really know how to deal with it. I was very quiet and had very little to say to my parents-in-law, and was always looking forward to the return of my husband on his day off. I remember my parents-in-law used to get up very early in the morning and I had to get up and cook breakfast for them.

Initially I had no idea what England would

look like. My first impression of England was that there were many houses and yet very few people. You had to drive for many miles before you could find a supermarket. Since I did not know my way around and my husband was not always at my side, I felt sad most of the time. I wrote to my mother a lot and told her about my feelings. My mother comforted me and said it would just take time for me to adjust to the new life in England.

My mother-in-law then found me a job sewing garments for a local factory which delivered the work to our home. I thus found myself occupied with the sewing work I had taken, and did not feel as miserable as before. I only learnt to use a sewing machine at that time. I thought if I learnt fast enough then I could make other changes for the better. However, I spent all my days staying at home and did not leave the house for many days. When my husband did come home, we would go for a walk or to the cinema. I never had any contact with other people except my husband's family.

Life here in England is very quiet and peaceful. English people just close their doors and there is no real contact at all between Chinese and English people. I did not talk to any English people during the first year I stayed with my parents-in-law. Later on I was delighted to hear from my husband that he had been allocated a council flat on the Lisson Green Estate after I became pregnant.

Since my husband lived in a private rented room in Chinatown at that time he made an application to the local council and managed to get rehoused by the City of Westminster in 1977. Ever since then we have been living in our three bedroom flat - for almost sixteen years now.

When I first moved to London I used to go with my husband to his restaurant every day. I stayed in a room above the restaurant and looked after my baby there. I did not know how to get around in London and relied on my husband, basically following him everywhere. I did not feel lonely or isolated at that time because I already had too much to do looking after my baby.

When I had my second boy, my mother came over from Hong Kong to help me. My mother actually found her way to Marble Arch and Oxford Street and she took me there for the first time. This was because I had introduced my mother to my downstairs neighbours, who happened to be a Chinese family, and Mrs Liu had taken my mother to see London - therefore my mother was actually showing me the shopping area! My mother stayed with me for six months, after which she went back to Hong Kong.

I then began to mix with some Chinese people whom I met in Church Street Market. We said hello at first and then later talked to each other. In 1981 a Chinese women's group was set up in the area so I met more Chinese people and made more friends. The Chinese women's group meets weekly and provides an opportunity for us to share experiences and give each other support. I enjoy coming to the group and meeting my Chinese friends.

After all these years, I have now made many friends locally. I often go to see them and we sit together and chat. Last week I went out nearly every day with my friends. Our husbands laugh at us for getting up so early every day and it seems like a daily routine for us to meet our friends; we were as keen as if we were going to work!

My two sons are 16 and 14 years old. The older one is studying 'A' levels and my younger son is still at school. Since my first language is Cantonese, I would find it difficult to help my children with their studies. Fortunately they are doing well at school and I have no need to worry about them. I always tell myself that I am lucky my children have never had problems with their studies and that I have never been asked to help, as I would be embarrassed at being unable to help them.

I did experience an incident of racial discrimination. It was Christmas time many years ago and I was taking my two children home by bus from Oxford Street. My two sons and I were sitting on three seats just at the back of the bus, next to the exit. When the bus stopped at Marble Arch, a middle-aged English woman got on the bus. She asked me whether I could read the English notice asking people to give up their seat to elderly people. I told her that my two children were only 5 and 3 and they needed to sit down. I offered to give her my seat but she refused to take it. She insisted that my two young boys should give up their seats to her and other people. She told the bus conductor and other passengers what she thought. Some people looked at her with approval but fortunately the bus conductor just ignored her. As I was standing up, my seat was then taken by another passenger.

When we got off the bus, I realised that this woman lived on the same estate as us. Every time I saw her again in the street she would come near me and mutter a few words at me. I tried to avoid bumping into her and would walk away from her if I saw her. Even now she still behaves like this after all these years. I feel that this is a typical example of racial discrimination.

Of course racial discrimination in England is quite a serious problem. I remember one member of our women's group who had some white English people queuing up behind her to pay in a supermarket and who called her a 'stupid Chinese'. I think if we can speak English we should respond to this kind of humiliation, otherwise such people will walk all over us and make life more difficult for us.

We do not have to be verbally abusive to show our anger and disapproval of this type of behaviour. The Chinese women's group can bring people together and organise sending letters to the appropriate bodies expressing our views. We need to work together constantly to combat incidents of racial discrimination; but we cannot expect things to change overnight.

The majority of Chinese people living here

at the moment do not speak much English. The language barrier makes life rather difficult. I think we should try to learn English and learn not to rely on other people. I have attended English classes, and manage to communicate using simple English. I would recommend that new immigrants coming to live in this country should learn to speak English.

Since I have already established my family here, it would be rather difficult for me to uproot again and return to live in Hong Kong. I have to consider my children first. I think I will only decide for myself when my two sons have become independent. I will certainly continue to live here for some years yet.

8. A newly born Chinese boy is named Peter Chan Tai-Man by his mother Yuk-King Man Chan. What is this boy's surname?

My name is LAU Lai Choi and I was born in East Africa on 2nd March 1946. I am now 47 years old. My parents had 15 children but my father had only one wife. There were 7 boys and 8 girls in the family and I am the youngest daughter. My father ran a grocery business in East Africa and my mother was a housewife. When I was two years old my family returned to live in Shun Tak, China.

I received a few years of formal education in China and then went to Hong Kong at the age of 9. Soon after we arrived in Hong Kong my father died and left all his businesses to my two eldest brothers. I continued my formal education in Hong Kong and finished at secondary school. Since our family business was doing quite well, life was comfortable for all of us. I remember we had servants to look after us and a chauffeur to drive us to school. We lived in one of the grand houses in Argyll Street in Kowloon.

When I was at school, I liked playing basketball, badminton and going to the cinema. I went to a Roman Catholic girls' school but the teachers used Chinese as the first language. After I finished secondary school, my mother died in 1965, and I spent two to three years studying English in Hong Kong.

I first came to England with my sister and her husband in March 1967 for a holiday. My brother-in-law was an Englishman and worked for the Hong Kong Government. He came back to England every year for a holiday. I joined them to see England, and travelled around

Europe for almost a year. When we were in Spain in April that year, we heard on the news that there were riots going on in Hong Kong.

When we returned to England, my sister advised me not to return to Hong Kong but to stay here and study nursing. My sister's in-laws helped me and another of my sisters to enrol for a two year nursing course (SEN - State Enrolled Nurse); I was 21 years old at the time. After I finished the course in 1969, I worked at a hospital in Kent for a year.

My impression of England was actually similar to what I expected from books I had read. The weather is cold, grey and gloomy, and makes people feel miserable. Particularly if you are all alone in this country, life would probably be unbearable.

A year later I came to work at Putney Hospital and lived in rented accommodation in Fulham. The landlady was an Irish lady who looked after me and my seventh sister. She sometimes cooked for us and invited us to join her for tea. Her hospitality made me feel warm and welcome in her house.

In 1970 my eldest brother came to London for a holiday. I joined him and his wife and moved to live in Hong Kong House at Lancaster Gate for a while. There were a lot of social activities arranged by the residents of the House for Chinese students who came from Hong Kong as well as professional people like nurses. I joined their photography club and met my husband there. My husband was working in the House as an assistant warden. We later

got married, in 1971. I was 25 years old at that time.

We had a church wedding and my two sisters attended the ceremony. My brother-in-law acted as one of the witnesses to the wedding. After we got married, we moved into the top floor flat in the same house in Fulham. I then stopped working as a nurse and worked with my husband for a travel agency in Chinatown.

A year later my husband and I started our own travel agency business in 1972. We then bought a three bedroom house in Harrow, in 1974. I had my first daughter in 1977 and a son in the following year, in 1978. We had to close down our business because there were quite a number of other travel agencies set up in Chinatown. We found it very difficult to compete with the others and my husband withdrew his share of the business and later found a job working for an American Insurance Company.

I then went back to nursing and started working as an agency nurse for a while. I got some temporary work and was later offered a permanent job working in a private nursing home for elderly people.

My first language is Cantonese but I also speak English. Since I was taught in Chinese when I studied at school, I had very little chance to practise my spoken English. I still found it difficult when I was doing my training as a nurse. I remember I had to carry a Chinese dictionary with me all the time to do my course work revision. It required double the effort to study here as English is my second language. Of course, there were times I thought about going back to Hong Kong, but I overcame the initial difficulties and my English began to improve gradually.

In the 1970s it was not so difficult to find a job in a hospital because there was a shortage of trained nurses. Nowadays it is a different story. You need to have the right qualifications and relevant experience before you can get an interview. On top of that you have to produce at least two references and your nursing registration number. Comparatively, it was much easier in my early days.

I have now been working for the same nursing home for the last sixteen years and I have not thought about moving to another job since I get on well with the staff and I am happy there. The people I work with are mainly English and I have never felt that there is any racial discrimination among the staff. However, some of the patients or residents of the home that I have worked with have shown disrespect to staff who are from the Black and other ethnic groups.

The majority of the residents in the home are over 80 years old. They still keep their Victorian values and think highly of themselves . They sometimes treat the staff like servants, shouting at us, and think that they pay for our jobs and therefore they are superior to us. There have been some incidents of racial discrimination. One of my colleagues is Black and has recently come to work in the home. Many of the elderly white people treat her badly, shouting at her for instance, and saying that they do not like her face purely because of her colour. Although this sort of thing does not happen to me, I still feel it is unacceptable to discriminate against people just because of their colour.

If that sort of thing ever happened to me, I would try to put things right by being assertive and would not tolerate any unreasonable behaviour. I remember one incident when a white resident in the home shouted at me 'You're foreign, go back to your own country'. This white man is well known to be a nasty and an unreasonable person. I reported his bad behaviour to our officer-in-charge. He was given a verbal warning and was told that he should not treat staff in such a bad manner.

All these years I have not joined any union or workers club because I never felt I needed to. The staff working in the home are just like family members and we have never had any conflict of interests that needed to be dealt with by a union. Besides, our home is substantially funded by charity and we get our salary increase every year without going through any official negotiation. Of course, strikes just do not happen there.

All my family members, except my eldest brother, are Catholics. I used to attend church every week but I stopped going to church for some years after I started working on shifts. Then in 1989 something happened which enhanced my faith in God. My daughter had a car accident that year when I was on holiday in Hong Kong. I prayed very hard and in the event she was actually not seriously hurt; since then I have attended church every Sunday.

Although I am a Catholic, I still celebrate Chinese New Year and give lucky money to my children. We also eat moon cakes at Mid-Autumn Festival. Since my parents' graves are in Hong Kong, it is rather difficult for me to pay my respects to them at Ching Ming and Chung Yeung. I also try to explain all the meanings of these Chinese customs and practices to my children.

During my spare time I like to help other people. Two years ago I went on a training course and applied to work as an interpreter for the London Chinese Health Resource Centre and Westminster Social Services. I help interpret for Chinese people who do not speak English at health clinics, hospitals, Housing and Department of Social Security Offices. I feel that I ought to help my own Chinese people in this country to solve their language problems, especially elderly people. I get a very good feeling each time after I have helped a Chinese person.

I am happy with my life and would not consider returning to Hong Kong, or anywhere else, as I am used to life in this country. I hope I will be able to live in comfort after my retirement and that my children will be successful in their lives.

9. Can you name two of the grand events in the Chinese New Year celebrations?

My Chinese name is TAM Kwok Man and my English name is Paul. I was born on 18th January 1946 in Hong Kong. My parents had 8 children and I am the eldest son in the family. My father was a civil servant and my mother was a housewife.

When I was 14, I was sent by my parents to study at a boarding school in Birmingham in 1960. I came to England by plane. I remember the flight took more than 24 hours and we stopped over in more than 4 different countries before landing at Heathrow. The schoolmaster came to the airport to meet me and three other Chinese students. We stayed in a rented room in Holborn for the night before travelling up to Birmingham.

When I first arrived in England, I found the place to be wet and gloomy. The buildings were old and run down. I found English weather rather cold and the food we were given wasn't enough to keep me warm. I was very homesick and wrote to ask my parents to let me return to Hong Kong. My parents tried to comfort me, saying that it would only take a few years to finish my studies and they did not really want me to return home because it would make them lose face in front of their friends and relatives if their son could not finish his studies. Since I had no friends or relatives in this country, I had to stay in the school during the holidays, but every now and then I would get permission from the schoolmaster to go out with other students to a Chinese restaurant for a meal. My parents had also sent me a rice cooker so that I could learn to cook for myself. I felt that it was only eating rice that kept me warm in the cold weather.

Fortunately all my expenses were covered by the Hong Kong Government due to the fact that my father was a civil servant. He was able to get three free air tickets each year, for me to go home, and I was able to see my parents very often during the first few years.

In 1967 I came down to London and worked as a clerk in a solicitor's office, as I wanted to become a solicitor. I found a bedsit in Streatham, south London. Since the solicitor's office was in Chinatown, I found my journey to work took up a lot of my time. I then moved to live in Hong Kong House at 74 Lancaster Gate in 1969. It was a hostel with more than 80 single rooms offering accommodation and providing breakfast for Chinese students. What I liked about the place was being able to have nice Chinese meals in the canteen. I lived there for another two years before I got married.

I met my wife in Christmas 1968 at a disco named 'Café des Artistes' in Earls Court. I often went there with the other Chinese students who were living in Hong Kong House, partly to meet new friends but really mainly to look for an English girlfriend. At the time we met, my future wife was working as a nurse in Putney Hospital. I invited my future wife, Harriet, to go with me to the Chinese church in Great Russell Street. I remember we enjoyed the service as well as the Malaysian food that was served at lunch time. Since then my wife and I have gone to the same church nearly every Sunday.

Harriet and I got married in November 1969. Before we got married we had been living together for a few months; I could say that we had already been 'living in sin' before the marriage. The reason we moved in together was that it was actually cheaper for us to rent a room together, as living in London was rather expensive. When I first started working in London, I earned about £2.40 a week. Of course, my take-home pay could not cover my living expenses and I had to ask my father to send me money from Hong Kong.

Another reason for me getting married was that I had problems with my student or trainee visa and the Home Office refused to extend it for me. I would have had to leave the country in January 1970. My employer, Mr Ising, advised me that it would save a lot of trouble if I was a permanent resident in England. Since I had always wished to marry Harriet, I decided to get married before Christmas. My colleague, Mr Wu, acted as a witness to our wedding, which was at Paddington register office. All my work colleagues attended the ceremony and later joined us for a drink in the pub.

Harriet is an English girl but her father is Irish and her mother is Welsh. We had actually got married before we told our parents and, of course, I was afraid that my parents would object to a mixed race marriage. Fortunately my parents seemed to accept my decision. Harriet's father came down to London from

York to see me the day after she broke the news to her parents over the phone. My father-in-law seemed to like me when we first met at Paddington station. Harriet and I also went to Hong Kong to see my parents soon after we had married. Since I could not afford to pay for the air tickets, my parents paid half the fares and Harriet's father paid the other half as a wedding present to us. Each ticket cost £96 at the time. It would have taken me a long time to save enough for the two of us to go to Hong Kong.

Our trip to Hong Kong was our honeymoon. When my parents met Harriet, they were delighted and I felt that they were very nice to her. I remember we stayed in a spacious flat at Castle Street in Kowloon, which my parents had specially rented for us so that we could stay as long as we liked in Hong Kong. My parents were afraid that Harriet would not like staying with the family since we lived in a very small flat at the time.

Harriet found that Hong Kong was very different from England. She felt that a lot of the Hong Kong Chinese were very impolite because she saw Chinese people spitting in the street and pushing their way to get on buses. She also noticed that some Chinese people went out walking in the streets with their pyjamas on. She told me that she would not like to stay in Hong Kong for long. Since I had already lived in England for more than ten years at the time, I had no plans to return to live in Hong Kong. We came back to this country after spending four weeks there.

Although I was lucky to have a job and work with English people, I did have difficulties mixing with them. Since English was not my first language, I sometimes could not pronounce a word properly and my employer could be quite sarcastic and would tease me about it. Of course, I felt humiliated at the time but I always kept quiet and acknowledged my mistakes. After a while Mr Ising came to think that Chinese people were very hard working and intelligent like himself - he was Jewish - and he later changed his attitude towards me. I had also gained a lot of trust and respect from him by working very hard and being loyal to the firm.

In 1970 I left the solicitor's firm to work in the High Courts as a clerk in Paddington and then became a civil servant. I changed jobs because the civil service job paid me better and Harriet and I had two young children by then. That was when I experienced many incidents of racial harassment. I worked as a legal clerk in court for more than 16 years but was never recommended to be promoted to the position of senior clerk. I felt that if you were not white your chances of getting promotion were slim. I left the job in 1988 and started a fish and chip shop with my wife, getting financial assistance from my brother-in-law. A year later we closed the business down because of the recession. I am now working in my brother-in-law's accountancy firm as an assistant accountant .

Of course, racial discrimination is quite a

problem in this country. Although I married an English woman, I know that not many of the older English people accept mixed race marriages. Harriet and I were always being stared at when some older white people saw us together at supermarkets in the late 1960s and early 1970s. I had also seen English people spit at Chinese people. Things have improved a lot now and we see many mixed marriages these days.

I have also asked my two children whether they have ever come across any incidents of racial discrimination. Maybe because they seem very English, they have never been discriminated against on account of being half Chinese.

My wife and I attend our local church, which is Church of England. It maybe because I am a Christian and have been living in this country for many years and married to an English woman that I have gradually given up most of the Chinese traditions and customs.

In my first few years of marriage, I mainly mixed with English people and hardly had any Chinese friends. That was until two years ago, when I began to mix with and meet more Chinese people through working for the London Chinese Health Resource Centre and for Westminster Social Services as an interpreter.

Through my contact with Chinese people living in London, I have noticed that a lot of Chinese men who work in restaurants like gambling. I suppose maybe they do not have the time to develop some heathier hobbies and they tend to see gambling as one of the entertaining things to do in their free time.

Personally, I do not like gambling. I spend most of my time wandering around London's antique shops and markets. I love collecting old coins, old books and so on - anything old interests me. I do not mind having second-hand goods, like furniture and clothes. There is a superstition followed by most Chinese people that second-hand or old goods bring bad luck.

I am a happily married man. My eldest daughter is 22 now and my son is 19. Through all these years I have got on very well with Harriet and believe I will continue to live in this country as I have no plans to return to live in Hong Kong.

However, following the death of my mother earlier this year, I feel I would like to go back to Hong Kong to live for a short time with my father, who is in need of comfort. I realise now that life is so short, and I regret that I have not spent more time with my parents, especially with my mother when she was alive. I am very sad that I did not have the chance to express my love and affection to her. I would like to be able to have more time to stay with my father and try my best to show him respect and return all the love that he gave to me throughout all these years.

10. Climbing up mountains on the Double Ninth Day is one of the many festivals celebrated by Chinese people and it is developed from ritual worshipping of ancestors. For most Chinese people what is the meaning of the number 'nine'?

Answers

1. Ching Ming has been one of the most popular festivities in China for thousands of years. People on that day go and pay respects to forbears at their tombs and go for outings. It is a day shortly after winter is over, a day in early spring, the season in which vegetation begins.

2. Twelve. They are Rat, Ox, Tiger, Rabbit, Dragon, Snake, Horse, Sheep, Monkey, Cock, Dog and Pig.

3. Cantonese and Hakka.

4. The City of Westminster. Chinatown, the social and commercial centre for the Chinese in London, is a part of the borough.

5. The Lunar Year or the spring festival is the most important traditional festival for Chinese. In Ancient China, the beginning of the year after the autumn harvest and winter storage and the time before spring ploughing and summer weeding. For farmers this was the time for relaxation and celebration after a years toil, time for looking back to the past and looking forward to the days to come, time for a good, long rest before going to the fields to do back breaking work again.

For many thousands of years Chinese people celebrated New Year to greet the new and pray for good luck. The keynote is renewal. The old year has gone with the misfortunes and wrongs, the new year comes and brings the opportunity for a fresh start. Socially, it signifies reunion. Personally, people in business hope to pay off debts, tidy up all loose ends and turn over a new leaf.

6. Bright red.

7. The moon is supposed to be brighter and fuller than in any other month and the moonlight is the most beautiful. In China, a full moon is also a symbol of family reunion and so that day is also known as the day of reunion.

8. Chan.

9. Lion dances and setting off firecrackers - for the purpose of keeping away evil spirits and exorcising ghosts, suppressing demons and seeking happiness.

10. The ninth day of the ninth Lunar month is the traditional Chong Yang Festival of the Chinese people. In ancient times, Chinese people regarded nine as a Yang or Kau or Jin numeral standing for good luck, happiness and a bright future.
This particular day with two Yang numerals is called double nine. Kau Kau or Jin Jin (nine nine) in Chinese is pronounced the same as the word 'long long' which is everlasting peace.

WONG Oi with her family

right: *LEE Lai Ping*

below right: *WONG Lai Ngor*
below: *YUE Kai Chung*

38

39

2

DESCRIPTION *SIGNALEMENT*

	Bearer *Titulaire*	Wife *Femme*
Profession *Profession*	*Chef*	
Place and date of birth *Lieu et date* *de naissance*	*Pindars Valley* *Clarendon JAMAICA* *29th September 1920*	
Country of Residence *Pays de* *Résidence*	*England*	
Height *Taille*	5 ft. 5 in.	ft. in.
Colour of eyes *Couleur des yeux*	*Dark Brown*	
Colour of hair *Couleur des cheveux*	*Black*	
Special peculiarities *Signes particuliers*	✓	

CHILDREN *ENFANTS*

Name *Nom*   Date of birth *Date de naissance*   Sex *Sexe*

CANCELLED

Usual signature *Franklin R Chin*
Signature du

Usual signature of wife
Signature de sa femme

3

Bearer
Titulaire

Wife
Femme

CANCELLED

(PHOTO)

Franklin CHIN's Jamaican passport

above: *WONG Yuen Tai with his daughter*

left: *WONG Oi and her family*

鳴　謝

本書的完成，首先要感謝西敏市社會服務署「橋華計劃」之主任麥武婉媚女士，她為本書搜集資料，訪問故事人物、轉錄記述、修正和翻譯錄音原稿。又多謝「口述歷史」計劃的負責人沙士喬治也古先生之協助、張雙明小姐提供的引導、與之感謝分別修正本書之英文及中文版本的顏文茲凡韋士先生和郭錦紅小姐。此外，更要感謝鍾太以無比的耐心完成本書的中文打字。同時，本人十分感激各故事主人提供引人入勝的生平故事。

最後，本書作者希望把此書獻給已世長辭的家翁及她的外子，更感謝她的外子一直以來給她不斷的支持和鼓勵。

本書的全部內容，均是各故事主人的親口敘述，筆者務求故事的真實性因而未加刻意修飾。有關書內所提及的評述意見，純屬故事人物的個人見解。

引　言

一八八零年代，中國海員開始在倫敦東區聚居，建立了一個華埠唐人街。而當時大部份居英華人是來自南中國的沿岸。當他們抵達英國沿岸的港口時，便決定留下。為了尋求更高的薪酬和更好的待遇，他們便註冊成為英國海員。

中國海員在倫敦東部船塢區定居下來後，不久便開設及經營洗衣店生意。他們就是以一雙手和少許金錢創造自己的事業。但是，這些早期居英海員都抱有一種 "過境" 的心態，一旦能儲蓄了足夠的金錢，便希望回到中國自己的故鄉。因此戰後有不少居英中國海員返回中國。後來，由於洗衣機的發明，洗衣店這個行業便漸趨式微。在迫不得已的情況下，那些留下來的華人祗好另謀生計到餐館裡工作。這使到華人移民英國進入另一個階段，也可說是一個華人以從事飲食業為主的年代之開始。

華人湧至英國定居是由兩個因素促成的。由一九五零年代後期至一九六零年初，英國的經濟突趨繁榮，人民生活質素提高，加上飲食習慣改變，他們崇尚外國美食佳餚尤其喜歡印度和中國菜。華人餐館業生意因而漸趨蓬勃，以至在一九五六和六十年間，移民數字不斷增加。而當時大部份移居英國的華人是來自屬於英國殖民地的香港之新界農村。

此外，由於當時有大量移民從南中國遷移至香港的新界地方，造成農地價格高漲，不少香港農民因而失去工作機會，於是他們決定往外地謀生。加上香港漸成工業化的城市，又因輸入大量中國農產品，造成香港農民更加難於維持生計。

與此同時，在一九六二年的時侯，英國實施了 "聯邦移民法例" 因而造成兩種現象，其一是英國限制在香港出生的華人入境，於是華人餐館便轉而聘請不受這條例限制的華人，而這些華人勞工大多來自中國南部。其二，因這移民法例的收緊，促使許多華人都盡早帶他們的妻子、子女和父母到英國團聚。

今日，華人社區的經濟資源是以飲食業為主，大部份的居英華人都經營餐館及外賣店，但亦有些華人是在香港長大和接受教育，有些則是來自馬來西亞和星加坡的留學生。所以他們都具有專業知識的。由於第二代華人都出生在英國，和在這裡接受教育，所以華人專業人仕也漸漸增加，他們也有意脫離傳統的飲食業從事其他的行業。

基於華人移民英國的經歷極具特色，加上一般英國人對居英華人缺乏認識，或者不多願意去加以了解，所以大部份英國人對居英華人都存有某些錯誤的觀念。例如他們把華人和"雜碎"食物和餐館連在一起。他們印象中的華人是樸素寧靜，自給自足，不願融入英國社會，在政治上不活躍，守紀律和性情內向。更甚地有些英國人還把華人與黑社會、毒品和賭博連在一起。

這些錯誤觀念已成為一種根深蒂固的思想，把居英華人的形象和特性定了型，英國人也因而忽略了社會和環境因素所構成的影響，漠視了華人社區所面對的真正問題和狀況。

這本書的出版，是嘗試更正這些錯誤觀念，讓第一代居英華人有一個機會以他們的語言敘述他們移民英國的經歷。並且為讀者提供一個機會去了解和認識今日居英國華人社區的面貌。

麥武婉媚

實事求事

我的姓名是黃堯泰。一九二八年七月十七日在香港出生。父親是商人和經營綢緞店生意。父親有三位妻子及六個兒女。我的第一位母親早死，二母有兩個孩子，而我的親生母親是排行第三。我有兩個親姊姊，一個同父異母的姊姊和兩個兄弟。

父親在我四歲時去世。同父異母的長兄與我的母親離開香港，返回中國台山。兩個長兄經營兩所商店，照顧一家。我在村中學校接受教育，直至十三歲完成小學課程。當日本侵略中國時，我所居住的鄉村受到一連串飛機轟炸，而當時留在台山縣是非常危險的，於是我和姊姊便逃往召關。我們步行了整整十六天才抵達一所安全的地方。十六歲時，我加入軍隊，希望為國家出戰，在軍隊內服役了三年。但是，我感到自己不適合軍旅之生涯，所以，我便返回自己的故鄉。我正式離開時剛也是戰爭結束。

二十一歲時，我到香港找工作。戰後中國人民生活艱苦，而許多人只為了兩餐的緣故，無薪酬都願替人工作。我在不同的店鋪工作，做過商店售貨員，廚師和中華航空公司工場的機械助理員。一九五零年，我開辦了一間名為安泰行的出入口公司，專經營出口外國生意。由於一九五一年美國及歐洲國家減少輸入外國貨，因此我的生意便一落千丈。於是就結束了自己的生意，加入一間有名的外國百貨公司--新樂工作。這間公司設有自己的商店、酒店和餐館。我由售貨員的職位做起，後來成為公司的經理。我是個用功和忠心的職員，而且能得到老闆的信任。在這份工作裡，我學習到不少的技能，也接觸到不同層面的人仕。

我的母親是一個虔誠的基督徒，而我亦受到她的影響，相信上帝。幼年時，經常與母親及姊姊到教堂。由於我需要在星期日工作，不能按時到教堂，所以，我己不像母親及姊姊一般的虔誠了。雖然母親不識字，但她能閱讀整本聖經。首位來英國傳教的教士李牧師，多年來是我家的最好朋友。

一九五八年，在香港遇上我的妻子，而我在三十一歲時結婚。我們的婚禮十分簡單，只是往婚姻註冊處註冊結婚，和邀請幾位朋友來吃飯慶祝。其後，在一九六零年四月三日我獨自離開香港到英國來。我已在這個國家生活了三十三年之久。我來英國是為了尋找新機會，因為一九六零年代，在香港許多中國人都難於生計。而當時，不是有許多中國人會喜歡來英國，因為他們認為這是一個貧窮的國家。

比較起來，如果你是去美國，中國人會羨慕你，因為美國一直被認為是一個金山，是可以賺到很多金錢的地方。許多人都告訴我，如果我來英國找生計的話，恐怕連薯仔也吃不到。

當我抵達英國時，我已感到在這個地方是個可以嘗試創一番事業的地方。我是乘船來到英國，而我儲蓄了足夠金錢支付船費。這段旅途長達一個月之久，而這亦是我生命裡的一個轉捩點。

我首先來到探訪一個曾與我在港一起工作的同事。她丈夫的生意遇上經濟危機而將會結束，他正尋找一個伙伴支持他的餐館生意。我表示會盡力幫助他們。他們非常高興我能出錢支持他們的生意。由於我帶了一些積蓄到英國來，所以我就成為他們生意上的合伙人了。我在廚房內當廚師，而我從香港那間百貨公司餐館內，工作所學來的廚藝也用得著了。透過我的努力工作，生意好轉起來，而在一九六二年我就收購了合伙人的另一半股權，成為獨資生意。一九六五年，我更在和京與朋友開設另一所中國餐館。

一九六九年，由於在生意上，我虧蝕了不少金錢，所以退出和京的生意，搬來咸密列開設一所外賣店。我已在

46

這區居住了二十二年之久，而我亦在和京經營了另一所中國餐館，有三年多。直至一九八一年，我們改裝這所外賣店，加建成為一所中國餐館。

我的母語是廣東話，但亦能說台山話和國語。因為我在香港學過英語，所以亦能應付日常會話。我感到英國人很仁慈，他們不會怪責我不能夠用英語表達意見。他們都會原諒我，因為他們認為我是中國人而英語又不是我的母語。當我不能用英語表達意見時，我會經常向他們道歉。有些英國人會認為我無需道歉，反之他們一點也不會說中文。我並沒有因為不能說流利英語而感到羞恥，因為我願意不斷學習，改善自己。

我對英國的印象十分好。我覺得英國人很友善和有禮。英國人都很實事求事，只要你肯勤奮和不做違法的事，在這裡為生是絕對沒有問題的。這個國家十分照顧市民，因為我們都享有免費的醫療服務及許多其他福利。這裡的免費教育制度也是非常好的。

六零年代，假如你是無家可歸的話，很容易可以入住一所政府屋。同時，如病了要接受手術的話，我們亦無須等候很長時間便可以進入醫院接受診治。懷孕的婦女也可得到妥善的照顧。當我的妻子來英與我團聚時，她帶著兩歲的女兒，我們亦得到免費牛奶。雖然這些優待現在已沒有了，但是教育制度仍是很好。那些來自貧窮家庭的孩子，他們不用支付任何費用，都能夠有機會接受高等教育。最難能可貴的是，這個國家會給每一個人有機會接受良好的教育。

初抵英國，我手持英國護照，入境經過移民局時，我沒有遇到任何問題。我覺得我在這個國家能夠好好使用自己的專長謀生。多年來，我沒有參加過任何工會和工人團體，因為我沒有多餘時間做這些的事。

居住在英國的華人都把自己視作他鄉

客。當然很多時我都有遇到種族歧視之事件，但是，我會保持緘默，避免提出這個問題。例如，有些英國人吃完餐後便毫無理由拒絕付賬。有些來中國餐館的英國顧客是很難接待且要求很高。我曾遇到一些英國人大聲呼喊和咀咒我，叫我返回中國，許多時，我都盡可能容忍這些行為。我認為我們需要避免麻煩和盡可能原諒他們。

另一個種族歧視的例子是我曾受到鄰居無理的捉弄。記得我第一次搬入自已購置的新房子，鄰居偷入我們的花園內，在所有的樹上鑽個洞。雖然我向警方報告，但我所得來的回覆是我需要有足夠的証據才可以舉報。許多時我的兒子在門前的花園玩耍，我們的鄰居都嚷著趕走他。他們更投訴我們在晚上發出很多吵鬧聲音。不管我如何去討好他們，送禮物和食品，我都不能與他們建立友誼。

居住在英國的華人，都很安靜和被動的，因為他們害怕惹上麻煩。華人在政治方面並不活躍，對於爭取政治權力不感興趣。在英國第一代之移民都會感到有些困難參與政治活動，因為他們大多數都沒有接受過教育。我只希望第二代或第三代的華人可以對於我們的權利和福利多些關注，或參加政治團體，去為華人爭取應有的地位。

雖然我身居外地，我仍追隨中國的傳統文化習俗。我們會慶祝中國節日，例如中國新年，我們會與餐館內的員工一起吃一頓飯和飲酒慶祝，互相祝賀。每年清明和重陽節我都會到母親墓前拜祭，我們會帶備鮮花，並且清除墓碑附近的野草。

我有六個子女。長子黃大衛是電子工程師。他於一九八一年回港工作，現是任職一間歐洲電子公司之營業經理。基於工作上的需要，他多次來往中國及歐洲，每年有三至四次來探訪我。長女於利茲大學畢業，是一位醫生。她曾在英任家庭醫生多年，與一位會計師結婚後，就與夫婿回港定居，現時她是國泰航空公司之職工醫生，婚姻愉快，亦育有一個女兒。

我的三女往美國加洲大學深造多年，現已完成碩士課程。四女是位藥劑師。幼女最近在卡地夫大學完成會計課程。幼子已十八歲，仍在修讀中學課程。

我覺得英國的教育制度能提供很多機會給那些有天份而又想進修的孩子，他們可以接受高等教育和發展他們所長。最好的是，無論任何種族和不同能力的人，都可以享受這裡的免費教育。

對我來說在英國教養孩子並不是件困難的事。我花了很多時間與子女一起，同時也費盡心血，盡力給他們最好的東西。我教導他們和解釋一般中國的傳統文化習慣。他們也會和中國人交往。

我希望子女可以成為社會上有貢獻的份子和能獨立生活。我把家庭放在第一位，努力盡丈夫和父親的責任。我所要求的是，子女能繼續成為社會上之正當份子，守法和有貢獻。

我並沒有計劃返回香港定居，因為我喜歡英國。中國人有句話 "久日他鄉為故鄉"。

49

心滿意足

我的名字是黃麗娥，今年七十二歲，出生於一九二一年五月十二日，原籍中國順德。我有許多兄弟姊妹但差不多都全在早年夭折。古時，中國人會盡量生養許多子女，如有一半以上的子女能夠生存，已算幸運，因為當時的嬰兒死亡率很高。我的父母有十三個子女而我是家中幼女。由於我在女兒中排行第四，所以我的乳名叫 "阿四" 。我不明白為什麼父親經常打罵母親，而母親還替他生下這麼多子女。我曾經問我的母親，為何她仍與父親睡覺，而又任他虐待。母親說我是個傻啞頭，問這些無聊問題。或許，母親真的很愛父親。

當我年幼時，父親便去世。由於家貧，我從未接受過任何正式教育，但是，我自己學懂認字。我雙親從來就沒有工作，而我的叔伯都是村中的大賊頭，一直是以打家劫舍來維持生活。從母親口中得知父親是個酗酒之徒，他沒有像其他兄弟以偷為生，只是向他們索取生活費。我還記得，我的叔伯常攜著手槍到順德沿岸碼頭，搶劫所有泊岸的船隻。

十四歲時，我開始替有錢人家工作，成為媒母，照顧孩子。當日本侵襲中國，我先逃到澳門後到香港。戰爭結束後，我替不少家庭做住家女傭。我相信年青時的我，是一個漂亮的女子，所以受到不少年青男子追求，可是當時我是相當高傲和挑剔，所以，從來沒有與任何人拍拖，沒有結婚。我亦是個相當勢利的女人，看不起那些勞工階層的男人。現時，想起來也有點後悔沒有結婚，和有個自己的家庭。或許， "沒有兒女一身輕" 總是好的。

在英國，我已住了二十六年。於一九六五年我與老闆來英，他為我買機票。我的老闆在香港擁有一間有名的商業銀行。我就是在這富有人家當住家女傭和照顧三個在牛津唸書的少爺小姐。我是他們倫敦住所的管家，我亦是負責清潔，煮飯和洗衫。我經常到牛津大學，給少爺小姐們帶些清潔的衣服和他們喜歡吃的食物。

首次到英國時，心情十分興奮。雖然我不懂說英語，但是得到老闆的清楚指示，已能自己認路到牛津。年青時，我的記憶力不錯，我相信自己是個醒目的人，學東西也十分快捷。有些時候我感到很孤單，但我亦因老闆肯帶我來英國而感到十分開心。

雖然，每年老闆都會買機票讓我回香港渡假，但我很少每年回港因為我覺得無此需要。其後，我再替他們多照顧兩個孩子。我對英國的印象相當好，英國之生活很寧靜和安逸。

雖然我不懂閱讀或書寫英文，但我仍努力學習認識一些常用之英文字。有一次曾經因不識看門牌而錯入男廁。我的朋友取笑我，但我認為這不是大問題，人做錯後才能學懂。

早年，居住在上海時，我已發現自己患有糖尿病。直到一九八六年，我的病情惡化，在家中浴室暈倒；事後朋友告訴我，自己在聖瑪利醫院昏迷了四星期。當我恢復知覺時，我失去了講話的能力，而左邊身體也不能移動。當然我不能夠再當住家女傭，反而需要他人照顧。我知道自己經過幾次開刀手術後才恢復知覺。幸好，老闆替我安排和支付住院的費用。住院六個月後，我的病情漸漸好轉和恢復行動能力。

離開療養院後，得到一位華人社會工作者之幫助，我得以安置在現時之政府房屋單位。感謝神，我仍能夠生存至今天。經過此次大病，我變成一位虔誠的基督徒，每星期日我都到聖馬田粵語堂做崇拜。

自從一九八八年至今，我居住在這個政府房屋單位已有五年了。初時的兩年，我靠自己的儲蓄為生，因我有二千多英鎊存放在房屋會內（即銀行戶口）。當我的儲蓄減少後，我就往唐人街之華人中心，要求工作人員替我申請福利金。現時，我以一些退休金和生活津貼金過活。

從來我沒有遇過種族歧視之事件，反而我感到英國人對我很好。我認為英國的小孩子有點頑皮，我指的是那些所謂 "壞蛋"，許多時，我所住的梯間有一班年輕小子會坐著一起，當我走過時，他經常取笑和騷擾我。雖然他們沒有向我威脅任何金錢，但他們總在區內造成不少胡鬧行為。有一天，我走過梯間，他們又再捉弄我一番，我即以扶手棍舞弄一下中國功夫給他們看。當然我也曉弄幾招，因為年青時我學過幾下功夫。當他們看到我的中國功夫藝術，表現得十分驚奇連聲叫好。自此之後，他們再也不敢取笑和走近戲弄我了，反而對我表現得十分友善。

雖然，在英國我沒有任何家人親戚。有許多朋友都肯幫助我。幾年前，我

在機場認識一位契仔。他現年三十歲，在唐人街餐館工作，當我病倒時我們成為好朋友。他已婚，育有兩孩子，他經常探訪和照顧我，替我做些家中修理工作，我就當他是兒子一樣，將來死後我會把我的儲蓄留一點給他。

我的鄰居也十分友善，我經常在街上跟他們打招呼。我喜歡住在這一區，也喜歡繼續留在英國享受晚年生活。這個國家對國民照顧周到，我享有所有權益和福利。有時我感到一個好的福利制度比養一個兒子還好，因為你知道福利制度會照顧你，而你不能保証你的兒子一定會照顧你。當然我會繼續住在英國。

說來話長

我的名字是陳凡基。在一九二零年九月二十九日出生於牙買加之加里當娜。父親有兩位妻子。其一為中國女子。父親在中國結婚後，不久便離開往牙買加，再與當地女子結婚，所以另一位妻子是牙買加人。我的親生母親是牙買加人，而我有一個兄長和兩個妹妹。父親在牙買加時是經營一間雜貨店，在一九二零年間，能夠擁有自己的生意，可算是相當富裕。

一九二八年父親托一位親戚把我和十歲大之兄長帶返中國，而他及家人仍留在牙買加。我和兄長回到父親原籍之廣東寶安縣，與父親之中國妻子和同父異母之兄姊共住。

中國母親對我和兄長有如親生子女一樣，我們相處融洽。兄長和我被送到村中之學校，接受了三年正式教育；其後，我們便在田中工作，種植自己的糧食。幸好我們能種植足夠的蕃薯來供養家中各人，中國母親亦把收割得來的食糧在市場出售以換來其他必需物品，如米和肉等。

一九三七年，日本侵略中國，我們一直享有之恬靜農村生活受到很大改變。恐怖之戰爭為中國帶來嚴重饑荒。中日戰爭期間，生活相當艱苦，僥幸我們一家都能夠生存。中日之戰長達十年之久，其間，我的中國母親與父親失去聯絡，而當時政府禁止所有市民書信來往。因此父親，無法知道我們在中國是否仍生存。

由於我在中國長大，我一直都跟從中國母親實行一般中國傳統習俗,例如,拜祖先和燒香。所以一點也不要驚奇的是，我是透過媒人認識我的太太。二十六歲時，我得到家人的安排與太太結婚。婚禮相當隆重，而我的中國母親也為我的婚禮花了不少金錢，因中國的傳統習俗是由新郎家人支付婚禮一切費用的。我們邀請了百多個村中之親友來參加我的婚宴。

婚禮是以中國之傳統儀式舉行，例如我和太太要三跪九叩來拜天地。由於我的父親不在中國，所有儀式都由一家之主的中國母親決定。

婚後，我和太太繼續居住在中國，在田中工作，以農務為生。太太為我生下一個女兒，可是當時生活貧困。一九四九年，共產黨取得中國政權後，我們的生活就更加艱苦。一九五七年時，由於中國政治局勢動盪，因此決定離開中國，找尋更好之將來。由於移民對共產國家來說，是一件不可能之事，我只好留下家人，逃離中國，經過驚險之逃生路途，翻山越嶺多日才抵達香港。當時任何難民一旦能逃至香港境內，都可獲准留下定居。抵港後，我到政府之移民局，要求他們替我尋找在牙買加父親之下落。在政府的幫助下，最後找到父親在牙買加之地址。

於是我便寫信給父親。父親回信，答允為我購買船票，好讓我能到牙買加與他團聚。可是，他當時並沒有經營生意，所以沒有經濟能力為我支付旅費。幸好聯合國把我當為難民，支付我往牙買加之機票費用。終於，在一九五九年我能往牙買加與父親團聚。

當我到達牙買加時，父親和我的親生母親到機場接我。很自然和可了解到的是，我非常高興能與雙親團聚。但是，當時我的父親已是個年邁而又身體衰弱的老人了。我亦同時與中國的妻子保持經常性的書信聯絡。我在牙買加居住了三年多，亦在不同親友所經營的雜貨店內工作，直至一九六二年才與當時一位僱主同來英國，到他新開設的雜貨店內工作。當時我需要自己積蓄足夠的金錢來購買來英國之機票，還記得機票之價值為八十英鎊。由於我持有牙買加護照，所以來英時無須領取任何入境証或工作准許証。很遺憾的是雙親於我抵英後不久在牙買加相繼逝世。

在嚴寒的一個正月天，我初抵倫敦東南部的新十字城。當時下著大雪，而我沒有帶來任何厚的預寒衣服，所以，我的僱主給了我一些衣服。英國的天氣實在與牙買加的天氣分別很大。在牙買加我們經常都可以享受陽光。我寫信到中國，要求妻子給我寄來一張綿被。當時，從內地寄來一張綿被之費用總比在英國購買一張更便宜。我與一位牙買加人同時在親戚所開的雜貨店內工作，我倆也支付少許的租金，在店鋪樓上居住。

多年來，我都與在中國之妻子保持聯絡，而我亦依時匯錢給她照顧孩子。一九六三年，中國文化革命後，大批人逃亡，我的妻子也離開中國到了香港。她在香港找到一份工廠工作，而我們的女兒亦交托中國的一位親戚照顧。在一九六九年，我返回香港與妻子見面，我回港之主要原因是為了與妻子在香港正式註冊結婚，以取回一張合法的結婚証書，以便日後申請她來英與我團聚。其後妻子於一九七零年來英定居。

於一九六八年，我遷往唐人街附近居住，同時在中國人經營的俱樂部做清潔工作。過去二十多年來，我的太太曾在倫敦以外地方替華人所開設的外賣店工作。由於她在倫敦以外很遠的地方工作，她只可以在放假的日子到倫敦與我一聚。

回顧過去，我很喜歡俱樂部的那份職業，因為那是一份清閒的工作，而且，我得到不少顧客的獎錢（小費）。可是，我的僱主一直沒有替我繳交國民保險費（即退休金）所以當我退休時，我並沒有權利得到任何退休金。

我的母語是客家話，我只能講少許廣東話和英語，但是，我能說很多的牙買加土語。我有許多牙買加朋友，他們住在倫敦而我亦經常與他們見面。雖然我有牙買加人的血統，但是我認為自己是一個中國人。多年在英國，我從未遇到任何種族歧視事件。我喜

55

歡與中國人交往，而我亦能與白種人和牙買加人相處融洽。

現在，我的女兒已婚和居住在香港。她育有一子一女。我和妻子經常回港探望他們。

我和太太仍實行一般中國人之習俗，例如慶祝中國新年及中秋節。現時，我們的社交活動多是探望朋友及玩客家牌。我亦有參加華人社區中心籌辦之老人會活動。有時，我的牙買加好友，哈頓會來探訪我，而我會為他弄一手特別菜式，因為他不喜歡吃中國菜，我煮的是馬駮魚炆香蕉。每三星期我都見到他，也會到他在碧士頓的家。

由於我不懂説英語，我便到唐人街之華人社區中心及西敏市社會服務署求助，要求他們替我處理一切申請福利金的問題。我覺得白種英國人對中國人很好，我認為有很多華人已安居英國，而華人社區並沒有存在任何問題。

我和妻子居住在唐人街附近之政府樓宇。英國政府已好好照顧我們，現在我們領取福利金而無須為金錢憂慮。我的妻子已六十三歲，而她十分的照顧我。我喜歡在唐人街附近居住，因為我可以較易見到朋友，方便到唐人商店買東西和參加區內華人社區中心舉辦之活動。

最近，我剛從香港回英。我和妻子逗留在香港有七個多月。我們都希望回到英國來，因為香港之天氣很熱和潮濕，而我們都睡得不好和胃口不佳。雖然，我的女兒及女婿對我們都照顧週到，和希望我倆留在香港，可是我們感到英國才是我們的家。我喜歡住在英國，因為這裡的天氣比較清涼，而我亦習慣了英國的天氣和這邊安靜及舒適的生活。相信我仍會留在英國生活下去。

入鄉隨俗，無拘無束

我的祖母給我取名為添娣，意思是希望我能帶來一個弟弟，而我父親則稱我為素霞。我在一九二零年出生於中國寶安縣。我的母親替父親生下六個女兒，而我出世後雙親更希望再生一個兒子。我是家中幼女，而我的三個姊姊早死，所以現在只有兩個姊姊。

當我七歲時，父親離開中國到星加坡（南洋）工作。母親也帶我的兩個姊姊一同前往，祇留下我一人。當時我大概十歲，和祖母同住。我出生於一個相當富有之家庭，一直都有一個妹仔（私人女傭）照顧我。

十一歲時，我入學讀書，接受了四年多正式教育後，雙親就沒有讓我繼續升學。我的姊姊，早在十二歲時被安排與他人結婚。我在五歲時亦早與一位男孩訂婚。

當我十五歲時，雙親由星加坡回中國。

他們向一個貧窮的家庭買了一個男孩，從此，我就當他是弟弟。雙親也買了一個妹仔照顧他。其後，雙親再返回星加坡居住。

二十歲時，我與未婚夫結婚。我是比較幸運能有機會與我的丈夫通信來往，互相認識。我們的婚禮是以西式禮儀進行，我穿上白色婚紗，在寶安縣註冊處舉行婚禮。

我嫁入了一個大家庭，而我的家公有三個妻子，即是我有三個家婆。在自己的家中我是個受到寵愛的孩子，不用做任何家務，一直得到妹仔照顧。婚後我經常流淚，因為感到丈夫之家人對我不好。他們只准我吃剩下之殘餘飯菜，要我做家中所有的雜務。當時之中國社會，女子只是二等公民，沒有任何地位。直到二十三歲時，當我產下一女兒，我便不再流淚自我憐憫，而變得堅強起來。

婚後不久，中日戰爭爆發。家人為了

逃亡而遷往南中國。戰後不久，大約在一九五零年代，共產黨在中國當權，所有富有人家都受到煎熬之痛苦。我和丈夫的家人都受到紅衛兵之虐待，因為我們被稱為 "有錢之大地主"。所以我們擁有的財產全被沒收，甚至祖母去世時，連棺木也沒有，無法好好的安葬她。我的弟弟幸好逃到南中國隱藏起來。當所有不幸事件發生時，我的雙親仍在星加坡。他們寫信告訴我，他們害怕回來中國。其後，我和丈夫替國家在田中工作，這才可以在那段時間得以生存。不久，我的丈夫找到一份在塔門教書之職，他於三十四歲時離開中國，到了香港一間鞋廠工作。於一九五七年我與兩個女兒前往香港與他團聚。

當丈夫在三十七歲去世時，我就變得更加堅強。當時我只有三十六歲，在一間工廠工作以維持生計。直到一九七六年時，我已五十七歲，才來英國。

我來英國與女兒同住已有十八年之久。

我仍記得初到英國機場時，飛機在早上三時下降，當日十分寒冷。我先到女兒家中居住。我不喜歡英國，因為自己一點也不會說英語，加上大多數時間只留在家中，替女兒照顧兩個兒女，為他們準備膳食。我的女兒和女婿出外工作，只留下我和孩子在家。對外面的世界，自己一點也不知道，每天只呆在家中，坐著等他們回來。大部份的時間，我都感到十分孤單和無奈。

直到十年前，自已學懂了到倫敦唐人街和上英文班。雖然，我仍不懂說流利英語，但是我能明白很多日常用的會語，而且我可以自已乘巴士，到雜貨店和街市購物。自從我的外孫長大後，我就開始到華人社區中心會見中國人。現在每天我都到唐人街參加老人會之活動。

我發現很難與新一代相處，感到居住在女兒家很不開心，所以決定搬出來到唐人街附近居住。我要求一位華人社區工作員給我意見及幫助。

去年一位華人社工幫我搬到蘇豪區來，替我找到屬於房屋協會之一房單位，而這個單位是屬於老人庇護屋。房屋協會更聘請一位會說廣東話的管理員來照顧居住在各單位之華人住客，而他也十分樂於幫助我們。

我的母語是廣東話，而現在懂說少許英語。我認為言語障礙對很多老一輩的居英華人來說，的確是一個極大的問題。我感到幸運，因為自己仍是很健康，相信對於老弱而身體有病的華藉老人來說，是有需要為他們發展有關服務。或許，需要在唐人街附近設立一所專給華藉老人居住的安老院。

多年來，我從未遇到種族歧視事件，而我覺得白種英國人對中國人很好。我的鄰居大多數是白種人，她們對我很好，他們時常來探望我，確保我是平安無事。我對他們的仁愛之心，表示感激。

自從來英居住後，我已沒有實行一般中國傳統習俗了。我再不刻意做年糕或燒香。我沒有感到在外國必須實行這些繁鎖之儀式，這裡的生活是較為簡單的。

我希望可以多見中國人和參加老人會的活動，我愛聽中國粵曲，在家中收集了不少錄音帶。我更愛好閱讀和練習書法。在空閒時間，我喜歡看中國小說，有時，我會到圖書館，借些中國錄影帶，更邀請朋友到我家中一同觀看。

我已在英國居住了十八年多，而亦看著兩個孫兒長大成人，了解到現今老一輩應多一點開放自己的思想及嘗試去接受新一輩的意見。我感到我們不可以用古舊的原則和思想教導孩子。我記得幼時需要聽父母的每一句話。我們已不可能強迫及要求新一代聽取我們的意見。我們需要有耐性對待子女，為了與他們相處融洽，有時還要聽聽他們的見解。

我喜歡英國寧靜和舒適的生活。現在我習慣了一個人生活。沒有想到將來返回老家中國居住，因為我會繼續留在這裡，在倫敦過下半生。

誠心誠意，竭盡所能

我的名字是黃愛，一九二六年六月二日在中國深圳福田村出生。我有三個哥哥和兩個姊姊。父母是以務農為生。我未受過任何正式教育，原因之一是自少家貧，其次因我不是男子，而當時中國人不准女子接受教育，而男孩則有機會進入學校讀書。正如所有農民的女兒一樣，我在田中工作和替家人看牛。

幼年時父母去世。日本入侵中國，我與嬸嬸逃到香港，當時我只有十一歲。一直與嬸嬸同住至十五歲。中日戰爭結束後，我便返回中國故鄉。但因戰後中國人民生活艱苦，所以我便再回香港謀生。其後，我在香港一間塑膠花出入口工廠工作多年。

透過朋友介紹，認識了我的丈夫。我們拍拖四年才決定結婚。當時本人已有三十歲。所以，我感到很幸運有權選擇自己的終生伴侶，不然的話便要經過媒人安排才可結婚。我們在婚姻註冊處舉行婚禮，且邀請一些朋友吃一頓飯作為慶祝。其後我倆往澳門渡密月。由於父母雙亡，所以我請求親友為我作婚禮的見証人。

我的丈夫是位鞋匠，在香港六零年代替人補鞋和造鞋。當中國輸出大量機器製成的鞋到香港時，造鞋業也相繼式微。我倆在五年間育養了四個子女，當時生活甚為艱苦，又賺不到足夠金錢過活。許多時，我倆只有捱饑抵餓，也要餵飽子女。就是在這種情況下，丈夫決意往外尋找生機。幸好丈夫的叔父是個行船水手，早年在英國東北部定居，他替我的丈夫申請了來英的工作証，並讓他在餐館內工作。於是在一九六四年我的丈夫離開香港，到了英國新堡市。他把每星期賺來的工資寄給我們。當丈夫到英國後，我和子女仍然住在香港島的一幢私人樓宇。後來，經過一次火災後，政府把我一家安置在柴灣的臨時木屋區。在那裡我們住了達四年之久。後來，我們得到政府徙置，搬往慈雲山。我們住在徙置大廈三年之久才移民到英國來。

一九七一年，我們一家離開香港乘機來英。我的丈夫只能儲蓄一半的旅費，而另一半是從表兄弟處借來的。記得這個旅程非常之長，大概在機上呆了二十多小時。對於這次旅程，雖然孩子們感到十分興奮，但在機上差不多每個人都有嘔吐不適的情形。

一家人抵達英國時，丈夫每星期只賺得七鎊。當時生活非常艱苦。我們一家租住一層房子，而每星期要交四鎊半的租金。孩子們的年紀是由七歲至十二歲之間，都需要我在家照顧他們。由於丈夫所賺來的工資不足夠支付一切費用，當孩子們稍為長大一些時，我便往外賣店做雜工。在廚房內做削馬鈴薯皮的工作，賺取每星期六鎊的薪酬。早上我送孩子到學校後便去工作。捱盡不少苦頭才可以賺取足夠金錢養活兒女。

我的丈夫曾在不同的中國餐館裡做助廚，從朋友中學習廚藝，漸進升為大廚。他替不同的親友工作，當他年紀大而手腳開始慢下來的時候，那時已無人願意聘用他，於是，我們便把積蓄了多年的金錢購得一間外賣店，經營家庭式生意。

我對英國的第一個印象是這裡天氣非常寒冷。初時，生活上有很多地方要適應。初期幾年我們經歷很多困難。也遇到種族歧視之事件，例如一些白種人大聲呼喝我們做"青期"，又向我們擲石頭，當時我們只有不作聲，盡量避免惹麻煩而盡快走開。由於我們不懂英語，而且又是居住在他人的國家，我們只好容忍。多年來，我只是遇到白種孩子的無禮捉弄，而從未遇到成年人以惡劣的態度相待。我相信是因為小童無知和缺乏教導，我們定要寬恕他們。

初期，因我不懂英語，所以感到很困難與他們交談。現在，在購物和乘搭巴士時我也能說幾句簡單的英語。

為了孩子將來有安逸生活，我一直都掙扎到底。子女現已長大成人，而他們也完成高等教育。長女與一位廚師結婚，育有兩子女，現時住在倫敦，每年夏季我都去探訪她們。

長子完成學位課程後，曾在醫院化驗室工作多年。他做化驗血液樣本的工作。他非常積極而又有進取心，三年前，他返回大學修讀物理治療科，本年六月他已完成這個課程，在新特倫醫院找到一份工作。我認為這個孩子非常聰明而又學業有成。他現時三十二歲，仍未娶妻。我希望他能快點結婚，我已經請朋友為他介紹中國女孩子。他忘於工作，似乎對於成家立室之事不感興趣。

次子大學畢業後在倫敦任職社工。這個兒子現在修讀晚間法律課程，他希望日後能成為一位律師。

我的幼女已完成大學課程，且修完一個碩士學位。在大學裡，她認識了一位從香港來讀書的男友，而當她完成學位課程時，便跟隨他回港。這位年青人，在香港是一位工程師，而我的女兒也在當地醫院服務，他們計劃在明年初結婚。

現在我不再擔憂了，因為我的子女已長大成人。一直以來，我都不需要勤加教導，而他們都能為自己將來計劃。這麼多年來，丈夫和我都是為子女而努力工作。我們希望他們有機會接受良好教育，所以竭盡所能給他們最好的東西。從來沒有要求子女在外賣店內長期工作，只希望他們把讀書放在第一位。我只希望他們無須擔憂金錢問題，而能夠謀生過好的日子。

僥幸子女都學業有成，我感到非常安慰。在眾多親友中，他們的子女在英國出生，但因讀書成績差而無機會入大學。其實，我為了子女的成就而感到十分驕傲。我經常提醒他們，只要

接受高等教育才能擴寬機會，可以脫離餐館行業，不用以勞力賺錢，都可找到較佳的工作。

我也經常告訴他們有關父母來英所經歷的辛酸。感謝上天，我的子女都是聽話和聰敏的，他們從來沒有與壞人來往，也能夠分辨好與壞。我深愛子女，仍會盡力引導他們走正確的方向。不斷支持和鼓勵他們。

丈夫和我於五年前出售了外賣店後才退休。我們儲蓄了足夠金錢，買下一所房子居住。憤憾的是，兩年前丈夫因肺癌去世，現只遺下我一人與長子同住，但我經常到倫敦富林區探望女兒。

我信奉佛教，且追隨中國一般的傳統習俗。例如：拜祖先和燒香。我仍雖堅持遵守我的信仰，但也讓子女到教堂，任由他們選擇其他宗教信仰。我們仍然慶祝中國新年，中秋節，清明和重陽節。自從我的丈夫去世後，每

年一家都會在清明和重陽到墓前，以鮮花恭奉以示孝道。在屋內，我在丈夫遺像前奉上一頓熱飯和燒香拜祭。家裡祇有我遵從這些儀式，我不期望子女做同樣的事，由於他們在西方文化長大，所以處事定會有所不同。我相信最重要的是，他們只要出自真心真意的尊奉，也不用一定要追隨這些禮儀。

在新堡市，我可算是老人會中的活躍分子。每星期我都參加老人活動，但因我患上腳部關節炎，行動不方便，最近已少參加這類活動了。

居住英國的華人都是勤奮和本著良心做事的。大多數華人都替中國人工作，很少會為英國人打工。早年來英之華人，雖不懂說英語，但很少華人會領取失業金，因為他們認為要英國政府來幫助是件羞恥的事，只有那些有病或年老而不能照顧自己的人才會領取福利以求生存；否則，很少中國人會倚賴政府的施捨。我認識的朋友當中，

他們很少會在六十二、三歲時提早退休和領取福利金，只有當他們因身體有病而不能長時間在餐館工作，才會無奈地向政府申請生活津貼。

有些中國人在六十歲後仍繼續工作，但他們的工資比年輕人少，因為他們不能夠做那些粗重的工作。大多數的朋友都會在他們五、六十歲前儲蓄一筆錢，購買一間外賣店，經營家庭式生意，動用家中大小維持生計。

第二代的華僑因能夠接受高等教育，所以可找到為英國人做事之工作；許多年輕的華人也許仍繼續經營家庭式飲食業生意。幸好的是我的四個子女是前者，不用再重操父母的故業。

現時，我領取一份寡婦退休金，生活也相當優悠，因為子女們經常給我一點錢作生活費。回顧過去多年，我沒有後悔移民到英國，因我們已能夠給子女們最好的機會。我也習慣英國的天氣和生活，我不會返回中國或香港

定居，因為我已老了不會活得多久。我希望留在英國過下半生，我也很滿意現時的生活呢。

千辛萬苦

我的名字是余介忠，生於一九二八年十一月十三日，今年已有六十五歲。出生地點是中國惠州。家中有十三兄弟姊妹，本人排行第四，亦是幼子。五歲時父母雙亡，我一直由長嫂照顧。長兄比我大十八歲，我視長兄長嫂為父母。

家中各人以務農為業，以種植蕃薯及稻米為生。家貧，自少未受過任何正式教育，所以連中文也不懂。九歲時，我替人家看牛，一直到十三歲，在長兄吩咐下回家下田工作。於十五歲時，有意去香港謀生，但途中遇到同鄉親友，他們都說我年紀實在太少，沒有人願意給我一份工作，於是我只有放棄行程回鄉去。

十六歲時，往雲南貴州替人家採冬蟲草，遇上我的妻子阿鳳。她是當地村長的女兒，而家境相當富裕。我知道她喜歡我，但因自己只是一個地主聘請的收割工人，不敢向她追求。加上我的身世寒微，與我一起也沒有將來。其實我也很喜歡她。

阿鳳經常到田來，遠遠偷看我工作。有一個晚上，我因工作過勞而染上感冒，她看見我躺在樹下睡著病倒的樣子，要求他的母親給我蓄著糖水充飢。其後，她更請我到家中與她們一家吃飯。當她的父母表示阿鳳喜歡我，並且要求我娶她為妻時，我感到非常尷尬和驚訝。當時，我不知如何答覆他們的要求，因為自己覺得太窮，配不上做他們的女婿，而且也擔心自己沒有能力給阿鳳豐衣足食的生活。

幸好阿鳳父母並不嫌棄我的清貧身世，認為我只要肯去工作，是不愁會餓死的。於是，我便提出帶阿鳳返回惠州拜見長兄，並且請求他准許我倆結婚。阿鳳聽了更欣喜若狂。當長兄見到阿鳳時，便一口答允了我倆的婚事，當時阿鳳只有十四歲。那個年代，男女都早婚，普遍青年人會在十三四歲時結婚。

我倆的婚禮是以拜天地和祖先為主，一切儀式在村中祠堂舉行。長兄也花費不少金錢，為我邀請了村中九十多位的村民來參加婚宴。婚後，阿鳳與我家人同住。我們分別住在不同房間，她住在磨房，我住在大廳，我倆當時年幼無知，不懂婚姻生活，也害羞去表達愛意。一直到十八、九歲才正式同床，行夫妻之禮，正式成為夫婦。

多年來我都是替長兄在田中工作，終於在二十歲時才正式離開惠州，留下妻子，自己到香港。我一直都希望可以離開鄉村，到香港見識城市生活。我帶了三斤白米，四隻鴨蛋，一雙草鞋。由惠州往香港，步行四日多才可到達；所以，晚上我便投宿茶莊，在露天長椅上睡覺。記得第一晚下著滂沱大雨饑寒交迫，境況悽涼。如今回想起初抵香港，無親無故，也忍不住內心的傷感眼淚直流滿面。

幸好遇上貴人容先生，他帶我到香港邊境之文錦渡。還記得當晚在他家中吃晚飯時，因多日未有飽餐，一味芽菇炆豬肉，我已吃得津津有味，大快朵耳，感到死也甘心。

初抵香港時，同鄉友人替我找到一份工作，在荃灣菜園收割。看到菜園裡的毛蟲在腳邊游來游去，真的把我嚇死了！大概在菜園工作了兩個月，便改上大冒山折竹枝到市場去賣，那時，生活是相當困苦的。記得，一束竹枝祇可賣得港幣三元（等於現今的三便士）。而當年儲蓄到七元便留起二元買米，把五元寄回中國給太太。

一九四五年，我抵香港時，第二次世界大戰結束，那時香港發生多宗暴亂，香港的國民黨黨員與共產黨爭鬧，令到人心茫茫。幸好港督葛亮洪處理得當，能控制暴亂，保持局勢穩定。

而我再也不靠賣竹枝為生，所以，四處找工作，到不同商店求職詢問。終於找到一份苦力，在地盆擔泥和跟車搬石。由於在地盆工作也相當辛苦，所以我便返回新界替人下田種菜。而我一直都與太太保持聯絡和匯錢給她。後來我儲蓄了足夠金錢，買下一塊土地自耕自足。

一九五二年，我的妻子和兩個兒子來港與我團聚。她不喜歡香港，後帶兩個孩子返回中國。而我繼續匯錢供養他們。

一位菜田地主鍾國良先生，欣賞我為人刻苦耐勞，聘請我到英國，在他的中國餐館工作。他是新界圍頭人，有許多田地，而且相當富有。以我所知，他更在英國開設多間中國餐館，希望在香港招聘人手。在我的同意下，鍾生替我申請有關文件及買了一張值三百四十鎊的機票給我來英國。終於在一九六四年初，踏足英國土地。

抵英後，我即到鍾生的中國餐館工作。初期的三個星期，我沒有得到半點薪酬，因為我只是學師仔。後來，則賺到一星期五鎊的薪酬。由於我不懂英語，所以每事都要倚靠別人，對我來說實在很難適應。雖然有想過離職返回香港，可是，我沒有足夠的金錢購買機票，所以，只有對自己說，留下踫踫運氣。

六零年代來英時，持有工作證的人仕都要經常到就近的警察局報到，而且還要取得批准才可轉工。我於一九六八年轉工。多年來我都是做廚師之職直到一九八六年病倒為止。由於我不懂中英語，我只有牢記菜單。幸好許多朋友都替我寫中文信以協助與中國居住的妻兒保持聯絡，直至妻子在一九六五年去世為止。但是，多年來我從未間斷過匯錢給她和兒子。

在英的生活，多是寧靜，但也是枯燥和呆板的。當我工作時，在放假天，我只是睡眠或往華人電影院看戲。由於我連中文也不懂，我實在很難學英文，所以我只可與中國人交往和替他們工作。我更很少賭掉薪金，因為我需要匯錢給我的家人；但是，有時我感到很慚愧，因為不能儲蓄足夠金錢返回中國，過退休生活。

我在五十八歲時提早退休，因為我患有嚴重的關節炎，不能工作。六年前我患病時，便被解僱，變成無家可歸。幸好得西敏市政府安置，和得到一位社區工作者幫助，得以入住一間政府房屋單位。我已居住區內多年，和領取福利金過活。

我對於現時在英國的生活感到很滿足，雖然，我在這裡只是一人，但還是比返中國好。因為，我不用擔心生活費而又有居住的地方。現在我正儲蓄金錢希望能回中國探望我的兒孫。我匯了一千鎊給兒子在鄉下興建一間祖屋，自己希望可以親眼看見這間房子落成。

我喜歡英國，因為這個國家照顧市民，我們享有免費醫療服務，老弱有病者能領取福利金過活。經過多年奮鬥，為了生活好，我不會離開這個國家。當然，在這裡有種族歧視，但是，我相信英國人對待少數民族已算很好。我們只是居住他鄉之客人，我們能得英國政府的照顧應存感激之心。因為在英國我已沒有任何親人，所以我現時大多數的時間都留在家中，很少用電話。社會服務署為我安裝了這個電話，是給我在危急之時可以聯絡到我的家庭醫生。我有很少的朋友而我又不怕單獨一個人留在家裡。多年來我都是住在唐人街，我對這裡很熟識，住在這裡可算十分方便。我會繼續留在英國直到我去世之日。

從頭至美

我的名字是李惠萍，一九二六年一月十日出生於香港紅磡。我的母親有十三個子女，但大部份都在幼時死去，而現時仍有七個生存。我是家中的大女。

我來自一個富裕的家庭。祖父於一九二零年代經營建築生意，他去世時，我只有六歲。祖父死後，我的父親沒有工作長達三年之久，他變賣了家中所有的財產，花盡了母親的積蓄，來維持生計。父親不甘願做低微而薪酬少的工作。因為他在香港一間有名的中學畢業，（名為華仁中學）所以他能閱讀及操流利中英語。可惜的是在他結婚後，就放棄讀書。

後來，父親在香港電燈公司內當檢查員之職。當時他每月薪酬有一百元港幣，算是相當不錯。母親是個家庭主婦，整天喜歡打麻雀而且是個好賭之徒。

由於祖父曾答允會讓家中的女兒有接受教育的機會，所以在我五歲時，便有機會到一間天主教學校讀書。第一天上學時，我收到不少由家人朋友和親戚送的禮物，我還要吃蔥頭，因為它代表聰明和智慧。家中有不少的傭人，他們都能好好的照顧我和其他弟妹，送我們上學。

接受了三年正式教育，我被迫停學，因為母親把所有錢賭光了，以至拒絕交學費。在校內，我的學業成績不錯，人人都稱讚我是個聰明女孩。放學後我喜歡與弟弟到不同的建築地盆玩耍。由於我經常都 "我行我數"，做自己喜歡的事，所以家人稱我為"小鬼頭。

十二歲時，我開始在表親開設的一間印刷工場工作。我是塗顏色的技工，把出口的聖誕咭塗上顏色。我在壹個月只賺得十五塊錢。我記得，自己把部份賺來的工錢給祖母買香煙。其實我害怕母親知道我這樣做，因為她要我把所有賺來的工錢交給她。

後來，我到一間製造塑膠鞋的工廠工作。由於我能閱讀和書寫中文，十五歲之年紀，我已被派當管工的職位，管理一班工人，而僱主也教我用算盤。我能計算簡單的賬項和工人工資。人人讚我是個負責和勤奮的工人。

一九四一年，日本轟炸香港。記得那天我在工廠正計算工人薪酬時，僱主吩附我們盡快離開，還給我白米，叮囑我們不要回去工作。

當日本佔據香港期間，生活相當困苦。我們沒有金錢也沒有食物，生活困難，因為一家大小人口多很難逃離香港。我記得日本軍人經常搜查市民屋宇，一天他們走到我家，為的是找英國軍人。幸好父親能說英語，說服日本軍人，解釋我們一家只是普通市民。而當他們看見我家有許多小孩時，就給我們一袋白米，好讓我們餵養小孩。我們把白米煮成白粥，吃了好幾天。

後來父親和我到啟德機場替日本人搬石頭，我們得到一日一磅白米作薪酬。我們只有燒傢俬以作燃料煮粥。回想這段戰亂時間，有三年零八個月之多，我們僥幸能生存至今，可算是奇蹟。

為了賺取多點白米，我亦曾替日本軍人做女傭；那時每月可得到二十四磅白米。假若不是這些白米，也許我們一家已餓死了！

一九四五年戰爭結束，父親找到一份在水務處的工作。我繼續替人家做女傭，又為英軍工作。於一九四七年，在英國軍營內遇上丈夫大衛。大衛是英軍，曾於第二次大戰在緬甸作戰，所以他能說些廣東話。當時，英軍是不准與香港的中國女子結婚。當他的上司知道他要與我結婚時，隨即就被調回英國。女兒未出世，他已離開香港了，當時我只有二十一歲。

我的父親見過大衛，也准許我倆結婚。可惜的是，我倆從沒有結婚，而我亦被這個英軍拋棄，多年來我都沒有與他聯絡。但是我曾在倫敦見過他一次，當時他已認不出我，而我也沒有和他打招呼。經過這麼多年，已沒有意思再與他有任何的接觸。

我自己一手撫養女兒成人。雖然，母親一直都勸我改嫁中國男子，但我相信這會對女兒不利，因為人家會把她當作私生女看待，而她因有西方面孔，是不會受人歡迎的。當時的年代單身未婚媽媽是受到人家的歧視，沒有人會可憐你，因為你會被社會遺棄的。

為了賺取多點錢，我曾在夜總會當舞伴。我離開這份工作，是因為黑社會的壞份子迫我當妓女。後來，我在九龍一所兒童院找到一份媬母工作。我喜歡這份有意義的工作，因為我照顧一群孤兒和幫助他們建立將來。我做這份工作有二十多年之久。

一九七零年，女兒與一位英國人結婚，來英住在都埤。一九七二年，我來英國與女兒團聚。我還記得在香港移民局接受面試時，移民官員告知我是我的女婿申請我到英國來定居，但我告訴他們我不大願意來英國，因為我怕改變我的當時生活。移民官員指出，縱使我移民英國，我亦可以隨時返港的。對於我的坦白，他們感到十分驚奇，他們安慰我叫我不用擔心。很快，我領取了入境証，進入了這個國家，長期居住下來。

當我抵達英國時，由於我的女婿，是英國軍人，他被調往星加坡工作兩年。這回，我拒絕與他們前往而決定留下來，與我的弟弟住在菝頓。後來找到一份工作，替一家星加坡來英之中國家庭做女傭，住在百定頓區。

由於我不懂英文，僱主經常吩咐我乘的士到唐人街購物，許多時拿著一張寫上自己住址的紙給的士司機以示我要到的地方。許多時，我遇到一些不誠實的的士司機，他們拒絕找回乘車後的餘錢。那時只需五便士便可以由百定頓乘巴士到唐人街。對於這些不誠實之的士司機我感到十分憤怒，於是我便下定決心學習認路和乘搭巴士。

過去十六年，我都為一家人當女傭工作，退休後，我便搬到尼臣堅區的一所政府單位。

我的女兒一家仍住在英國，我的女婿已離開軍隊，現為英國電視台工作。我還給了他們一萬三千鎊去購買一間屋，我經常探訪三個孫兒，還帶他們到唐人街吃點心。

我已在這裡居住了二十年之久，我喜歡英國，因為在此我不會受到歧視。六十年代，香港華人不接受異族通婚。我的兩個妹妹都與英國人結婚，而後母亦是位白種英國女士。我無須隱瞞自己的背景，可以坦白講述自己的生平事跡，而不會被人取笑。

在英國，我認為種族歧視不是一個嚴重的問題。我和英國鄰居相處融洽，也到附近的老人關懷中心與他們玩泵波拿。大部份的時間，我都花在逛街和探訪朋友。每星期，我可領取退休金過活。對英國的生活，我很滿意，在此我會繼續活完下半生。

事在人為

許多人都稱呼我為文太，一九五五年出生於香港。家中有五兄弟姊妹，而我排行第四。父親是一名文員而母親是個家庭主婦。我家住在大嶼山多年而後期則搬往香港島居住。

七歲時入學，修讀至中學二年級。由於我對讀書不感興趣，所以十五歲便停學。我的興趣是籃球和美容化妝。少時志願做女警，但因父母反對而放棄這個念頭。離校後，我在不同商店當售貨員。

有關我來英之故事，實在說來話長。一直以來，我從未想過移民英國，直至遇到現時之丈夫才有這回事。一天，姊姊告訴母親，她的一位朋友之家人從英國到香港密識妙齡女子作過埠新娘。這位朋友之父母想替兒子找一位中國女子為妻，而他們是在英國經營餐館生意。現時之奶奶，文太透過不少朋友取得幾張女子照片給其兒子選擇。對於這種擇偶方法，我的丈夫一點也不感興趣。

母親和姊姊曾想到我，也問我可否把我的相片給這位文生看看。聽說他是專程到香港尋找年輕而又想嫁到外國的女子。當時我只有二十一歲，沒有拍過拖，也不想離開父母。但父母又認為我已是到了合適年齡要找個終身伴侶的時候。由於我沒有反對他們的提議，所以他們就拿我的照片給了文先生。自此，沒有聽到父母提到有關照片的事，我就完全忘掉了這回事。

一天，母親帶我去見文太太和她的兒子。或許這叫做一見鍾情，我與他談得十分投契。在場的每一個人都看得出我倆均喜歡對方。同時，我亦感到他是個很容易相處的人，也承認很喜歡他。很自然的事自此我倆便見過多次面。原先，我的丈夫不願意見那些由他母親介紹的女孩子。他在十二歲時來到英國，已經變得很西化，但他的母親不希望他娶鬼妹為妻，所以才堅持要介紹女孩子給她。

很奇怪，我倆很喜歡對方，經過了一段很短的拍拖日子（只有一個月），丈夫便向我求婚。於是，我倆在婚姻註冊處結婚，和安排了一個只供親戚朋友參加的婚宴。當我倆決定結婚後，丈夫向移民局申請我到英國與他一起。當時丈夫是替家人管理餐館生意，不能長期的留在香港。

其實他可以先回英國，等我領取了入境許可証才來與他一起。但是，一切事情都進行很順利，兩星期內我便領取到入境証。所以，我便與他一起離開香港。或許整件事情發生得很快，我沒有足夠的時間考慮到自此便離開香港了，而我一直沒有任何感覺，直至在機場離別的那天，與母親説再見時才突然流下淚來。當踏上飛機時，內心感到十分矛盾和擔心，才省覺到以往的一切事情都由他人替我安排，而沒有機會讓我説不好。這個改變實在太大，是自己沒有細心考慮到的。

由於我從少在家中受到疼愛，多年來得母親的適心照顧，所以，突然間自己感到很害怕和憂慮，擔心自己能否適應英國的新生活。

在一九七六年，到達英國時，我與老爺奶奶同住在費頓，丈夫在倫敦工作，每星期他只可以回來與我相聚一天。這對我來説，實在是個很大的轉變，而我也不知道自己是否適應得來。自己性格很靜，也很少與老爺奶奶説話，而每天只盼望丈夫放假回來。記得每天老爺奶奶都很早起床，而我也要一早起來，弄早餐給他們。

最初，我一點也不知道英國是個怎樣的地方。自己對英國的第一個印象是這裡有很多屋和很少人，你需要駕車好幾哩才可以找到一間超級市場。由於自己不識路而丈夫又不在自己身邊，很多時我都感到不開心。我經常寫信告知母親有關我的感受。母親都安慰我，還説只要過一段時間，就會適應英國的新生活。

後來，奶奶替我找到一份工作，是在家中替人車衣，我家附近的一間工廠負責車送衣物給我縫製。於是，我便花了所有時間在車衣工作上，而不感到像以前般的不開心了。其實，那時是我第一次學用車衣機。我相信如我能學快些的話，我就能夠為將來打算。可是，我就花了所有的日子留在家中，有時好幾天我也不會出門，當丈夫回來時，我倆就會外出散步，或到戲院看電影。除了丈夫家人以外，我從來沒有接觸其他人。

英國的生活是十分寧靜和平安的。英國人經常關上門，而中國人和英國人是完全沒有接觸的。記得在第一年到英與老爺奶奶同住期間，我從未與西人説過話。後來知道丈夫在倫敦申請到一間政府屋，我簡直欣喜若狂，當時我己懷有身孕。當時，由於丈夫租住唐人街附近的一間房，所以在一九七七年時，他向政府申請安置，得到西敏市政府安排遷來這區。至今我已居住在這所三房一廳的政府房子達十六年之久。

初遷到倫敦時，每天我都到丈夫的餐館，躲在餐館樓上的一間房子內照顧我的嬰兒。我不認識倫敦周圍的地方，只依賴丈夫帶我出外，每一步都跟著他。因為照顧嬰兒已令我忙過不停，所以我完全沒有孤單的感覺。

當我產下第二個孩子時，母親由香港來幫我。母親竟比我先知道如何到馬布亞和牛津街，她更帶我去。原來我曾介紹母親給樓下的鄰居認識，他們都是中國人，而廖太曾帶母親遊覽倫敦，所以母親曉得往牛津街購物區。母親只住了六個月便返回香港。

自此之後，凡在街上遇見中國人，我便開始與他們打招呼。初初只是打個招呼，後來就談起話來。一九八一年，在區內我們成立了一華人婦女會，我遇上更多中國人，也就結識了更多的

朋友。華人婦女會每週聚會一次，我們有機會分享經驗和彼此支持，我喜歡這個小組和認識的中國朋友。

經過這麼多年，在區內我認識不少朋友。我經常探訪他們，大家一起傾談。上星期差不多每天我都和朋友外出。丈夫還笑說我像返工一樣，每天都見朋友。

我的兩個兒子分別是十六和十四歲。現在大的一個修讀預科，而小的一個還在念中學。由於我的母語是廣東話，所以在幫助兒子學習時，我遇到不少困難。幸好，他們在校的成績不錯，所以我都不用擔心。我覺得自己很幸運，因為兒子在學業上沒有遇到困難，所以他們從沒有向我問功課上任何的問題，否則，我定會感到十分尷尬。

我曾經遇到種族歧視之事件。許多年前的一個聖誕節，我帶兩個兒子乘巴士到牛津街購物。回程中，我們坐在巴士後尾的三個座位，當巴士在馬布

亞停站時，一位中年英國女士上車，她問我是否懂得閱讀 "讓位給老人" 的英文表記，我指出因兩個孩子只有五歲和三歲，所以他們需要一個座位，而我同意讓出自己的座位給她。但她拒絕我的提議，而堅持要我讓出兒子們坐著的座位給她和其他人。她並向其他乘客和售票員提出她的理由，有些乘客表示讚同，但售票員沒有理會她，而我讓出的座位亦很快便被別人佔坐了。

當我們下車的時候，才知道那中年女士是住在我居住的區內。自此之後，每次在街上遇到她，她都故意走近我的身邊向我說些不客氣的說話。而我為了盡可能避免踫到她，所以每當遠遠看到她時就快快走開。直到現在，她都是表現出很不友善的樣子。我覺得這正是種族歧視之例子。

當然在英國種族歧視也算是個嚴重的問題。記得婦女會的一位成員曾遇到一些白種人無禮對待。她在超級市場排隊付款時，站在背後的白種人叫她 "愚蠢的中國人"。我相信如果我們能懂說英語的話，對於這些侮辱我們一定要作出反應，否則，那些人更會得寸進尺，令我們更難在這裡生活。

我們毋須用粗言表達出憤怒的情緒，和對他們的行為表達不滿。華人婦女會應該齊心合力寫信給有關部門，以表達我們的意見。除非我們合力堅持抵抗種族歧視事件之發生，否則這些事情不會有所改變。

現時大多數居住英國的華人都不懂說英語。言語障礙的確令生活上遇到不少困難。我相信我們定要嘗試學習英文，而不要倚賴別人。我曾上英文班，學懂了與人溝通的日常英語。我會提議新來英國的移民去學英文。

在英國，由於我已建立了一個家庭，要我改變現時的生活，返回香港實在是件不容易的事。首先，我要考慮到我的兒子。我會在兒子長大自立後才為自己著想，我會繼續留在英國，多住幾年。

安居樂業

我的名字是劉麗彩，在一九四六年三月二日出生於東非洲。今年四十七歲，父母有十五個子女。我有七個哥哥和八個姊姊，而我是家中最年幼的女兒。父親在東非經營雜貨店，而母親是個家庭主婦。當我兩歲時，一家返回中國順德居住。

在中國我讀了幾年書，九歲時便到了香港。抵港不久，父親過世，留下了所有的生意給兩位長兄。在香港，我繼續接受教育，直至完成中學課程。由於生意經營得當，我們的生活相當優悠。記得家中有傭人照顧我們更有一位司機接送上學。我們居住在九龍亞皆老街其中的一間富麗大屋。

讀書時候，我喜歡打藍球，羽毛球和看電影。我在一間天主教女子中學讀書，但所有老師用中文教學。我於一九六七年完成中學課程，母親亦在當年逝世。之後我在香港修讀兩年至三年英專。

初次到英國是在一九六七年三月，我與姊姊和姐夫來歐洲渡假。姐夫是英國人而他是政府公務員，每年他都會回英渡假。我與姊姊一家人遊覽歐洲各地差不多一年。同年四月，當我們在西班牙，從新聞得知香港多處發生暴亂。

返英國後，姊姊勸我不要回去香港，提議我留英進修護士科。得姐夫的親友介紹，我和七姊註冊修讀護士課程，當時我只有二十一歲。於一九六九年完成護士課程後，我在倫敦南部的一所醫院工作。

我對英國的印象正如我從書本得知一樣。天氣寒冷，天色灰暗，令人悶悶不樂，心情憂傷。尤其是單獨一人生活在這個國家，更感到留英生活並不好受。

一年後，我轉到倫敦的畢尼醫院工作，在富林區租住一間房。房東太太是愛爾蘭人，她悉心照顧我和七姊，許多時，她會為我們預備晚膳，還邀請我們與她一起共進晚餐。她的熱情款待，令我們感到不少溫暖。

一九七零年，大哥來英渡假，我與哥哥嫂嫂一起遷往蘭加士達基的香港屋共住。那裡有不少為來自香港的留英學生和專業華人安排的社交活動。我參加了那裡的攝影學會，因而認識了我的丈夫。當時，我的丈夫是香港屋的行政管理員。我們於一九七一年結婚，我當時是二十五歲。

我們在教堂內舉行婚禮，我的兩個姊姊也來參加，姐夫還為我作婚禮的見証人。婚後，我倆遷回富林區那所居住過的房子。我不再當護士之職，而與丈夫一同在唐人街的一所旅行社內工作。

大概一年後，即一九七二年，丈夫與我開始經營旅行社生意。七四年，我們在哈勞區購置一所三間房的屋子。七七年，我生下女兒。七八年，又添個兒子。由於唐人街多間旅行社成立，我們的生意大減，而在激烈的競爭下迫於要結束旅行社。丈夫出售股權，後替一所美國保險公司工作。我也返回護士行業，替一間薦人館工作。首先在一間老人療養院當替工後成為院內之長期護士。

我的母語是廣東話，而我也懂說英語。由於在中學時，學校是以中文教學，所以我很少說英語。因此在受訓為護士期間，在學習上我遇上不少的困難。由於英語不是我的第一語言，我便要加倍努力學習。我記得經常要拿著一本中英字典來溫習。當然，有時我也都會想回香港，但我能克服最初的障礙而我的英文也漸有進步，所以後來再沒有這樣的想法了。

一九七零年期間，由於大多數英國的醫院都缺乏護士，所以找一份工作不算困難。但在今天就不同了，你要有合適的學歷和有關經驗才可有面試機會，而且你還要有最少兩份推薦書，並且要有註冊登記護士的証明。相比之下，在那個年代，找工作是比較容易。

過去的十六年，我都是在一間療養院工作。因為我在那裡工作愉快，而與其他職員相處融洽，所以我從來都未想過離職。所有與我一起工作的都是白種英國人，我沒有遇到種族歧視的事件。但是居住在療養院的老人或病人對某些黑人或來自少數民族的職員，都曾有表現出種族歧視的態度。

大部份居住在療養院內的住客都是超過八十歲，他們都持有維多利亞年代的價值觀和自視很高，當職員是工人一般地呼呼喝喝，以為他們支付我們的薪酬，便可以高高在上的鄙視我們。有些情況是與種族歧視有關。職員當中有一位是黑人而她也是初來步到，許多白種老人都對她不好，例如大聲呼喝她，也說她的膚色不同，所以就不喜歡她。雖然，這些事情並沒有發生在我身上，我認為因膚色之不同而歧視他人是一種不能接受的行為。

如果此類事情發生在我的身上，我是會爭取自己的權利而不會容忍不合理的侮辱。記得曾有一位白種住客向我大聲呼喝說:「你這個外國人,返回妳的國家去。」這位白種老人是位出名難相處的住客，我將他的惡劣行為告知院長。院長就口頭警告，告戒他不可以重覆同類的惡劣行為來對待職員。

多年來我沒有參加任何工會，因為我覺得無此需要。在院內工作的同事好像一家人，我們從未遇到某些情況是需要工會人員替我們出頭解決。同時我們的療養院是一所資源充足的慈善機構，每年都無須經過任何爭辯便得到合理的加薪。當然，我們從來沒有嘗試罷工這回事。

除了長兄，我們一家都是天主教徒。我經常都到教堂，多年前因我要返輪班工作，所以便停止到教堂。直至一九八九年發生了一件事而加強了我信主之心。當年我的女兒遇到一宗車禍，而我那時身在香港渡假。我懇切禱告，幸好女兒沒有受到嚴重傷害，自此，我便每星期日到教堂。

雖然我是天主教徒，我仍慶祝中國新年和派 "利是" 給兒女。我們也在中秋節吃月餅。由於父母的墓地在香港，所以我難於在每年的清明和重陽節去掃墓。我盡可能向子女解述一般之中國傳統和習俗的意義。

在空餘時間，我喜歡幫助他人。兩年前我參加了一個訓練課程，替倫敦華人保健中心和西敏市社會服務署做傳譯工作。我在醫院、診所、房屋署和社會服務署為中國人作傳譯。我感到我們需要幫助居住在英國的華人，尤其是老人家，解決言語上的困難，每次我幫了中國人後，內心都有舒服的感覺。

我對於現時居住英國的生活感到滿意，而沒有想到返回香港或到其他地方居住。多年來，我已習慣了這裡的生活，只希望退休後能夠生活安定，而子女也能自立成人。

敢怒而不敢言

我的中文名字是譚國民，而英文名是保羅。我於一九四六年一月十八日在香港出生。父母有八個子女而我是家中長子。父親是位公務員，母親是個家庭主婦。

一九六零年，當時我只有十四歲，父母把我送來伯明翰的一間寄宿學校讀書。我是乘飛機來英國的。記得飛機在四個不同的地方停留，行程超過二十四小時才抵希斯路機場。學校校長到機場接我和其他三個中國學生。我們留在倫敦渡宿一宵才前往伯明翰。

初到英國時，我覺得這是一個又濕又悶的地方。所有的房屋都非常殘舊。英國的天氣十分寒冷而學校提供的食物不足以預寒。當時我很思家，所以我寫信給父母要求他們讓我返回香港。父母安慰我，指出只需幾年的時間我便可以完成學業，他們不准我回去，因為這會令他們在親友面前丟瞼。由於在英國我沒有朋友及親人，所以每逢學校假期，我都留在學校內，有時校長會准許我與其他中國同學到中國餐館吃飯。父母寄來一個電飯煲，好讓我可以學懂煮飯。我覺得只有吃飯才可以在寒冷的天氣下保暖。

幸好父親是政府公務員，我的學費是由香港政府支助的。每年我有三張免費的機票回港，所以最初的幾年我都可以經常見到父母。

一九六七年，因為我希望成為一位律師所以我到倫敦一所律師行工作。當時我在倫敦南部支咸租了一間房。由於律師行是在唐人街，所以我每天都花不少時間在返工的路程上。其後，於一九六九年我遷往蘭加士達基的香港屋居住。香港屋是一所學生宿舍，專提供住宿和早餐給留英的中國學生。(宿舍內有多過八十個房間)我喜歡香港屋是因我們可以在飯堂內吃到中國餐。婚前我在香港屋居住了兩年多。

於一九六八年聖誕，我在愛閣的一所的士高認識我的太太。我經常與居住香港屋的中國同學到這所的士高，其實我們到那裡是想找個鬼妹女朋友。當時我的太太是在畢尼醫院做護士。我邀請我的太太哈妮華與我到碧屈素街的華人教會做崇拜。記得我們十分喜歡那裡的崇拜儀式，也喜歡崇拜後在教會內享用馬來式午餐。自此之後差不多每星期我和太太都到那裡做崇拜。哈妮華與我在一九六九年十一月結婚。在我們結婚之前，我們同居了幾個月，可以說，婚前我們已活在罪中。我們同住的原因是因為倫敦的生活費相當高，其實一同租住一間房是比較便宜。當初我在倫敦工作時，每星期只賺得二鎊四十便士。當時我的薪酬是不能夠應付生活上的開支，所以我還要請求父親從香港寄一些錢來資助我。

另一個結婚的原因是我的學生工作証到期，內政部拒絕給我續期，而我要在一九七零年一月離開英國。律師行的僱主，艾誠先生提議假若我是長期居民那麼可免了許多麻煩，他便不用替我向移民局每年申請延期。由於我一直都想與哈妮華結婚，所以，決定在聖誕前了件心事。我的同事胡先生為我做結婚的見証人，而我們在百定頓的婚姻註冊處結婚。所有律師行的同事都有到來參加我的婚禮，禮成後我們到酒吧喝一杯慶祝。

哈妮華是英國人，她的父親是愛爾蘭人，母親則是威爾蘭人。我們沒有預先通知父母有關我們要結婚的事，婚後我們才告訴父母。其實我是很害怕父母會反對這段異族婚姻。幸好我的父母接受我的決定。在我倆結婚的第二天，哈妮華的父親便從若克郡到倫敦來見我。我的外父初次在百定頓火車站見到我時似乎都喜歡我。婚後不久，我和哈妮華一同回到香港見我的雙親。由於我沒有能力支付機票費用，所以我倆的父母各支付一半費用，作為我們的結婚禮物。當時每張機票為九十六鎊。我要儲蓄很久才能有足夠

的金錢支付兩人回港之費用。

我們以回港作為蜜月假期。當我的父母見到哈妮華時，他們十分高興，我也感到他們對哈妮華十分親切。記得父母刻意為我倆租了一所位於青山道的大房子給我們居住，並說可以住到離港為止。當時因為我們所住的地方很陝窄，父母恐怕哈妮華不會喜歡與我的家人一起同住。

哈妮華認為香港實在與英國有很大的分別。她感到香港人沒有禮貌，因為她見到中國人隨地吐痰，而且爭先恐後上巴士。她也看到一些中國人穿著睡衣在街上走來走去。她說不希望長期居住在香港。當時，由於我已在英國居住了十年之久，又沒有計劃回港居住，所以我們逗留了四個星期便返回英國。

雖然我很幸運與英國人一起工作，但是我亦有困難與他們混在一起。由於英文不是我的母語，有時我的英文發

音不大正確而我的老闆會取笑我。當然我感到有點被侮辱，但我只有不出聲或承認自己的錯處。經過一段時間，艾誠先生明白到中國人刻苦耐勞，又像他猶太人一樣聰明，他就改變對我的態度。其後，因為我一直都很努力工作和忠心於公司，所以得到他的信任。

一九七零年，我離開律師行轉到百定頓高等法院任職文員，當時我是一位政府公務員。我離職的原因是因為公務員的薪酬不錯，加上我和哈妮華育有一子一女。我經歷到不少種族騷擾的事件。在法庭工作了十六年，我從來沒有機會被提升做高級文員。我感覺到因為自己不是白種人，所以升職的機會很微。一九八八年，我離開這份法庭職位，得到妹夫經濟上的支持，與太太開始經營一所炸魚外賣店。一年後因生意不好而結束。現時我到妹夫開設的會計師行內任助理之職。

在英國，種族歧視可算是相當嚴重的問題。雖然我與英國人結婚，但我知道許多老一輩的英國人不會接受異族通婚。在六、七十年代，哈妮華與我在超級市場購物時，受到不少年老的英國人以不友善的眼光注視。我也親眼看見英國人向中國人吐口水。現今已有很大的轉變，我們可以見到很多異族通婚的例子。我曾和兩個孩子提及這些種族歧視事件。可能由於他們的樣子像英國人，所以從沒有因是半個中國人的原故而受到歧視。

太太和我仍到區內附近的教堂做崇拜，此教堂是屬於英國國教。可能因為我是基督徒，同時在這裡居住了多年，而太太也是英國人，所以漸漸地我放棄了許多中國人的傳統習俗。結婚初期，我主要是與英國人混在一起，並沒有中國朋友。直到兩年前，我替倫敦華人保健中心和西敏市社會服務署做傳譯的工作，便開始接觸和認識到更多的中國人。

我接觸到不少居住在倫敦的華人，發

覺到有很多在餐館工作的中國男子都喜歡賭錢。我相信他們可能沒有時間培養健康的嗜好，而他們認為在空餘時間內，唯一可以消遣的活動就是賭博。

我本人不喜歡賭博。平日，我經常逛倫敦的古物店和市場。我喜歡搜集古老錢幣和舊書，而任何古舊的物品都會引起我的興趣。我也不介意買 "二手貨"，例如傢俬和衣物。大多數的中國人都很迷信，他們認為用"二手貨"或古老的物品會帶來不好運。

我是一個婚姻生活美滿的男人。大女兒己是二十二歲而兒子也有十九歲了。這麼多年我與太太哈妮華相處融洽，相信我會繼續住在英國，也沒有計劃會返香港居住。

但是，自從年初母親去世，因為父親需要別人安慰，所以我便希望可以回港與父親居住一段短時間。我了解到生命很短暫，也後悔當母親在世時，自己沒有好好與父母相處過。我感到很難過的是，因為沒有機會回報母親對我的愛心和關懷。我希望可以爭取一些時間與父親相處，盡力去回報他多年來對的照顧和支持。

86